The Inspired Workplace:
Organisational wisdom from the most unlikely of sources

The Inspired Workplace:
Organisational wisdom from the most unlikely of sources

Matthew D Henricks

Henricks Consulting Pty Ltd
2016

First Printing: 2016

ISBN: 978-0-9946199-0-7

Henricks Consulting Pty Ltd
34, 42 Wattle Rd
Brookvale, NSW, 2100
Australia
www.henricksconsulting.com
+61(0)2-8061-3918

Ordering Information:

Special discounts are available on quantity purchases by corporations, associations, educators, and others. For details, contact the publisher at the above listed address.

For my nephews Heath and Noah.
Two little men born with a special purpose.

TABLE OF CONTENTS

INDEX OF STORIES

PREFACE

I believe that most of us in the developed world live an incredibly sheltered existence. We read the Harvard Business Review, subscribe to a few blogs and corporate newsletters, throw in a dose of YouTube and convince ourselves that we possess a truly worldly perspective. If our perspective happens to trend on social media for 24hours that is sufficient endorsement to render our opinion fact and we move onto solving the next first world problem.

But what if our media sources didn't even scratch the surface? What if the collective wisdom of the majority of people on earth was not accessible to us? The reality is that we live in such a world. Only 40% of people in the world have access to the internet to share their views. The other 60% obviously have only a limited ability to be heard. The majority of those people also live in poverty on less than $2.50 per day. Even if they did have access to the internet, these people are frankly too busy working to survive and provide for their families to be distracted by world events or be a "part of the conversation" online. What if the most inspiring leaders in the world were not even part of the conversation?

During my time working on charity projects around the world I've met numerous people living in poverty. Frankly, many of them are amongst the most inspiring people I've ever met. If you want to believe that you have a truly world-view, if you want to truly be an exemplar of best practice then as a bare minimum, you should understand the way the other half lives. Better still, if you open your heart to their stories I think you'll be truly inspired.

For the first 10 years of my career I worked exceptionally hard. Frankly, I probably worked too hard. I almost revelled in the unhealthy amount of stress that I was able to tolerate and my life was completely out of balance. I prioritised financial, work and career-related goals above anything else and as a result my personal and family life really did suffer. During that time, I felt like I was moving forward and getting ahead yet the truth was, I was sleep-walking through life. Sure, my eyes were open to commercial hurdles and opportunities, but they were firmly closed to my heart's deepest yearnings.

Several years ago, I got involved in a charity project that forever changed the course of my life – the Helping Hands Program. I share many stories in this book about the people that I have met in developing countries as a result of that program together with our latest project, Water Works. Typically, in each story I share, I am the one travelling overseas to provide a life-changing gift to someone in need. However, each time it has turned out that I have been the beneficiary of the most beautiful and unexpected gifts and insights. Gifts that would ultimately change the course of my life and deeply impact on my practice as a leader.

I believe that many of us have lost perspective in life and especially at work. We often get caught up in the day-to-day excitement of the workplace and forget about what's truly important. I believe that when we lose perspective in that way nobody wins and we usually make poor decisions as a result.

This book is an opportunity to reflect on a range of stories that will put things back into perspective. I believe that not only will these stories help you strive towards a more balanced life, they will also help you make better decisions at work. If you read this book with an open heart and allow yourself to be inspired by the stories within, I believe that you will be one step closer to leading and shaping an inspired workplace.

I.   THE FUNDAMENTALS

This section explains some foundational concepts that the rest of the book is based on. I start by exploring one of the core beliefs that this book is predicated on; that each and every person was born for a reason. We then describe the charity projects that have inspired this book, namely, the Helping Hands Program and Water Works Program.

Finally, this section finishes by explaining the power of perspective and how opening your heart and mind to a completely different view of the world can often have a profound impact personally and in your practice as a leader.

Chapter 1: Born to change the world

If you're like me you were born with a naïve sense that you were put on this planet to do something special. That the world was going to be a better place because YOU personally were in it. You were still just a kid, a babe in the woods, but you knew that when your time came, you were destined for amazing things. Sure you might have seen how hard your family members worked, you might have even noticed the odd hiccup or two in their lives, but you would learn from them, avoid as many as you can and NOTHING would stand in your way.

It's one of the things that make us innately human. We are all born with that wide-eyed and innocent sense that we are special. It might have been a long time ago for some of us. Maybe you've forgotten the small details of your dreams as a kid but if you really try and remember a time before fear, before day-to-day life took its toll, before school or your first family member passed away chances are, like me, you can remember this time where there was no doubt in your mind that you were destined for something amazing.

Of course there are a number of factors that lead to some of us clinging to those dreams a bit longer than others. However, I firmly believe that we are all born dreamers with big hopes for the future. That naivety we are born with is there for a reason. It's that childlike wonder that makes us stretch to the stars. If you think about it from an evolutionary perspective it might be that one characteristic that's enabled us to get to the point we have as a species.

Sadly, most of us let life slowly but surely strip us of our biggest dreams. Maybe you missed out on a promotion. Maybe a teenage romance didn't work out and you've always wondered what might have been. Maybe your job is really busy and you don't have time for dreaming. Perhaps you noticed a nemesis having success or a loved one experiencing failure. Whatever the process involved, most of us only allow our inner child to come out and dream after we've had a glass of wine and fallen asleep after battling another day.

What if it didn't have to be that way?

This book is written on the assumption that one of the constant pulls on our heart as people is a desire to recapture the dreams of our childhood. This book is written based on the assumption that we are ALL born to do something incredible and that the world IS a better place because each and every one of us is in it. So if you don't know WHY you're here yet, or if you haven't recaptured that childlike naivety recently then your heart is likely longing for a change of pace. I hope this book can help you reconnect with your dreams and find your true purpose.

If after reading this chapter you don't believe there to be a shred of truth to it then this is not the book for you. However, if you're looking to be inspired again, if you look around your workplace and see a bunch of people that are also looking for significance then I invite you to go on a little journey with me. Let's go a bit deeper together and as Morpheus says in the matrix – "let's see how deep that rabbit hole goes".

Sadly there are 3 billion people sharing our planet that are just like you and me except that they live in poverty. That means they get by on less than $2.50 per day. I believe that each and every one of those people was born EXACTLY just like you and I. They also believed that they were born to do something incredible. Chances are, many of those people are the same ones that were stripped of their childhoods much too early. Some of those people live in societies where they are taught from a very early age that they are not equal. Maybe their politics is unpalatable. Maybe they happen to subscribe to the 'wrong' religion. Maybe they were born with or acquired a disability. Often people living in poverty have been taught to keep quiet, to only speak when they are spoken to. Often people in poverty have learned to be invisible…

This book is written based on the assumption that those same people who have learned to be invisible also deserve to have the kind of dreams that we share. In fact, those same people are some of the most inspiring people in the world. This book will share the stories of the most inspiring people that I've ever met from around the developing world. I believe the process of reflecting on those stories will help you take the next steps in your leadership journey. I believe that if you just listen to some of the stories that I'll share in this book not only will you be inspired but you'll hopefully regain the courage to dream again yourself - to recapture your inner-child and go out there and be extraordinary.

A byproduct of the success of this book is that you'll not only be empowered to take your leadership practice to the next level, you'll also be helping to fund the work that we do in our charity projects Helping Hands Program ™ and Water Works Program ™. Each of these projects essentially starts with an audacious belief that we CAN abolish poverty in our life-time. None of those 3 billion people in the world deserve to be living in poverty but without the right kind of help, climbing out of that predicament can be impossible. Each one of these books purchased will either help people with disabilities in the developing world or people who don't have access to clean water in Africa. Either way, your purchase of this book has helped in a small way. Although throughout this book you're going to be learning some important lessons from some of the poorest people in the world, you're also going to be making a difference for that same group of people.

Perhaps there are people reading this book that have decided they were born to be ordinary. They are wrong. In fact, they could not be further from the truth. We are all potential leaders. We are all incredibly special. We are all inspiring. The purpose of this book is to enable each of us to live an inspired life and create an "Inspired Workplace".

Chapter 1 – Key Insights

- We were each born to do something significant in the world.
- Most of us have convinced ourselves that we were born to be ordinary but this couldn't be further from the truth.
- The same can be said of people who life in the developing world. In fact, they are often the most inspiring people in the world.

Chapter 2: How a boy from the suburbs in Sydney met the most inspiring people in the world.

I'm the first to admit that I've been one of the lucky ones. I was born into a loving family living in one of the richest nations in the world. I've had the ability to get a good education and up until five years ago was running a highly successful Human Resources Consulting firm. I was very good at being a consultant and had surrounded myself with some exceptionally talented people. We were all making plenty of money and business was growing strongly. Things were going really well... except they weren't. Something was missing.

Of course when you run your own company there is always going to be a baseline level of motivation involved because you understand how closely related your effort and reward are. It's true that when you work for yourself you can take time-off whenever you want to. However, it's also true that there are very few business-owners that I know who take this opportunity. There is just too much to be lost by taking leave at the wrong time; and it's always the wrong time. Of course there's a difference between just "existing" at work and truly being motivated. Although I hadn't taken a holiday in several years I didn't feel as though I was achieving my life's ambition by any means. It's true to say that although starting up my own firm was exciting at the time, several years later the novelty had worn a little thin and I was looking for something else to get back that "spark" that I once had. I'm not ashamed to say that I was even toying with closing the business and applying for another corporate job at that time.

During our working lives I think we all come across people that have an unarguably positive influence on our careers. Sometimes just one interaction with the right person can leave a lasting impact on us. Other times, the people that have the most influence on our career development will weave in and out of our lives in different forms for many years. One of those people for me is an inspiring woman named Colleen Cuthbert. She is both a past manager, client and friend who constantly challenged me to take my practice as a consultant to the next level and as luck would have it I happened to be working with her during my time of disorientation career-wise and I was considering a career change.

The year was 2011 and I'd been working on a project with Colleen for some time. Although the bulk of my assignment was complete, she was gracious enough to invite me along to a leadership event that in some ways was the culmination of the project we'd both been working on for 12 months. I gratefully accepted the invitation. I've never attended an event that Colleen has run which hasn't been incredibly engaging and challenging on every level. Needless to say I arrived with a sense of anticipation and wasn't let down.

During that event we had an opportunity to experience a workshop called the Helping Hands Program and Colleen whispered to me during the activity that there was no Australian-based distributor for the program yet. My interest was piqued immediately but I was also

8

felt more than a little conflicted. You see although I had a fairly varied background I had never seen myself as a facilitator or Learning and Development expert. In fact it was probably the aspect of my practice as a Consultant that was the weakest. Despite that reticence, Colleen has a way of inspiring people to stretch beyond their comfort zone and before I knew it I found myself meeting with another guy that happens to be one of the most inspiring people I've ever met - Bill John of Odyssey Teams.

I met Bill in the lobby of the Four Points Sheraton Darling Harbour in November, 2011. I can still remember the meeting now – walking tentatively into the lobby of a major hotel and looking around for someone that looked "American" who might also be looking for me. Once we found each other I think it only took us about five minutes to connect and establish a rapport. It was another five months after that (and a number of successful programs) before Bill invited me to be the distributor of the Helping Hands Program within Australia and New Zealand. I had NO idea what I'd just agreed to do. I wasn't a trainer, and had no existing networks to sell the idea into. I didn't have the first idea how to get started but I was incredibly inspired by what Bill and his team had already achieved globally with the initiative. I think it was that passion that tempted Bill to take a risk and partner with me. Despite not being clear about the best next steps, all of a sudden that sense that I was just "existing" at work evaporated. I didn't just feel inspired about the challenge that was ahead of me but it was probably the first time in my life where I felt like I was exactly where I was meant to be. I think that I had rediscovered that boyhood dream of mine to make a difference in the world and there was no way I was going to let that dream be taken away from me this time!

The Helping Hands Program™ is essentially a corporate team building and Corporate Social Responsibility activity that enables workplaces to build and donate real prosthetic hands to people in the developing world (sadly many of these people are also landmine victims). For those that haven't had an opportunity to attend one of our events (yet), we bring along 30 pieces of plastic and metal and then your employees physically assemble a real prosthetic hand that is going to change someone else's life. It sounds like an overwhelming challenge and it is. That's the way that most attendees feel when they start an activity, but as they work together with their peers eventually they find that the challenge isn't quite as hard as they initially thought and by the end of a 2.5 hour session every single group will typically have been successful.

Many of us have had the displeasure of attending a tired old leadership and team-building program. Maybe we build a human pyramid, catch a trembling colleague who is sweating profusely, then retire to the lobby of a hotel to debrief what we've learned. Well Helping Hands is different. There is a real product involved (the hand), there is a real customer out there (about 1 million people in need globally that cannot afford to buy a hand themselves), those customers have real quality requirements, there are real time-frames and a few curveballs. In every sense Helping

Hands is less of an "activity" than most. My favourite thing to say is that we are "inviting each participant into our business for two hours and our business is every bit as real as theirs". Effectively, customers are "in business together" it's just a different kind of business than they are used to.

Following the activity, not only have we changed someone's life, but we've got an extraordinary amount of insight to share as a team about the way we worked together. About the difference that having a sense of purpose has on the way you approach your work. There are a myriad of other topics we discuss during our workshops and attendees get a lot personally out of the experience. However, more importantly, wind the clock forward a few years and we've now built 7,530 hands in

A new hand recipient

Australia alone and globally we've built over 27,000. For more information about our program check out www.helpinghandsprogram.com.au

The Helping Hands Program has been much more than a workplace activity for me. I've thrown myself into all aspects of the project. Not just running it as a leadership and team-building activity but also getting involved in distribution of the hands themselves. Initially, my involvement in distribution was motivated out of a desire to be able to talk with authenticity about the kind of difference the hands make overseas. However meeting one little boy during my travels was enough to shift my perspective and broaden my interest in the project.

It was the end of 2013 when I went on my first trip to Cambodia to help fit some of the hands we had made. Up until that time we had relied entirely on a registered charity, The Ellen Meadows Prosthetic Hand Foundation, to distribute our hands for us but I felt that it was important that I see some of the people that we were helping first hand so that I'd have some personal stories to share with our clients back in Australia. During that trip I met a young boy that was born with no arms or legs due to Agent Orange contamination in the soil his parents farmed in. This was a boy that was born with no arms and legs but could hold a pen between his forearms and write his own name more legibly than most doctors. He could also run at a fairly brisk pace with the help of legs that had been donated by another charity organisation. Our job was to provide him with two new hands. It's hard to explain how moved I was to meet this young man. I remember instantly feeling guilty about the kind of things I'd worried about when I was his age; school, girls, pocket-money and sport. It all seemed so petty in that moment. This kid wasn't just born without arms and legs he was helping out around the home, getting an education and at the same time helping his father farm a small plot of land. In the moments after I met that child I knew that my involvement in the Helping Hands Program would never be the same again. I'm not embarrassed to say that I feel almost as if this project is a personal crusade. I'm unashamedly zealous about our work with the hands because I can see the difference that our project makes. My primary role with the Helping Hands project is to run corporate workshops that help people see the world from a different perspective. However, the passion that shines through during those workshops has never been the same since I met that little kid who was born with no arms or legs.

The Water Works Program™ is the second charity project that we have so far gotten involved in. In 2015, after about four years running Helping Hands we were starting to get an overwhelming demand from our clients for another charity-related experience. They had built hands last year and were looking for something equally powerful but different this year. So we spent 12 months researching the various world-wide charity projects that we might be able to partner with. It was important that we didn't just find a need that was indisputable, but also a project that would translate well into a team-building and leadership activity. Furthermore, it was really important to us that we found a great charity partner that understood their project inside and out. We didn't want to re-create the wheel, we wanted to partner with a registered charity that would look after all of the operations for us.

The project that we settled on was a clean water project because during our early research it became incredibly apparent that the need for clean water is perhaps the biggest problem in the world today. About 1 billion people in the world do not have access to clean water and sanitation. Each and every one of those people are unnecessarily exposed to completely avoidable water-borne diseases. The kind of diseases that we are talk about range from dysentery, cholera and a range of other issues that would not be difficult to cure with the right medical treatment. However, tragically in many parts of the world, the right medical treatment simply is not available and the people are left treating only the symptoms... often with the same dirty water that made them sick in the first place. In the developed world we wouldn't treat our pet animals as poorly as this, yet world-wide, half of all hospital beds are taken up with precisely this kind of avoidable illness. Beyond that, many of the people that are exposed to the highest risk wouldn't have access to something that most readers would recognise as a "hospital bed". Tragically, people are perishing every day due to these completely avoidable water borne diseases.

As with every huge global problem it's fair to say that the solution is unlikely to be simple. Rather, there are a large number of different projects needed and over time, together as a global community, we can fix this problem for good. The best known types of projects that addresses the need for clean water are bore-drilling (i.e. water well construction) projects. If water well is drilled to the correct depth by skilled professionals the quality of water that is extracted from the well is typically a big improvement on the other water sources available to local people. The other great outcome from a new water well is that the water supply is almost limitless and one well can provide sufficient water for an entire village. There are of course a number of problems with wells. Not all well water is perfectly pure so there is always a risk associated with drinking untreated ground-water. This risk is magnified during floods or heavy rains. However, there are a number of other practical issues associated with such projects. Often water can become contaminated during the process of transporting it from the water well to the home. This can easily happen through the use of unhygienic water vestibules or through poor hygiene practices during water handling. In addition, although one well might provide sufficient water for an entire village, walking to the well and back is often a 5 kilometer (approximately 2 mile) journey. One final problem with well projects is their placement within the community. Of course it's always critical to speak with local community leaders whenever you are considering a new charity project. Those community leaders are meant to speak on behalf of the best interests of all community members however the sad truth is that sometimes there is bias involved in the choice of location for a new well. Not only can this result in many members of the community having to travel long distances to reach the well, often the route required can be treacherous and during our travels we have talked to people who refuse to drink well water because of past experiences being assaulted on the way to their local well.

Of course ground-water projects are a critical part of the solution to this terrible global problem but clearly they are not the entire solution. During our research we also came across a number of charities which provide water filtration systems to local people. These filtration systems obviously don't solve the problem of transporting water long distances, but effectively it means that if people can only gain access to water that is unsuitable for drinking then they can at least filter it once they get it home. From our investigations we found a number of different filtration systems available however during our travels we tragically also came across many such systems that were broken or in a state of disrepair. Water filtration systems, when working have some significant benefits relative to ground-water projects. One of the most significant is that they can typically be used as both a filtration and storage solution at the point where each family needs to use water (their home). Another significant strength of all filtration systems is that they come at only a fraction of the cost of drilling a new bore-hole.

For the Water Works Program we decided to partner with an amazing organisation called LifeWater. They provide probably the simplest, tried and tested filtration system on the market. The system can be assembled in a purely mechanical way which is a real strength as the local people often don't have the skills or tools required to fix the solar-powered, electrical models we have seen in the field. The LifeWater system using a ceramic filtration candle which effectively screens out all bacteria, parasites and other impurities down to half a micron which is incredibly small. The technology was first commissioned by

Queen Victoria and has been in use for decades. Better still, it's cost effective and cheap to install. If it breaks it's also easy to fix locally.

Within the Water Works project, we don't just assemble a real LifeWater filtration system, we give participants an opportunity to test the way it functions. Can you think of a more personal way of ensuring quality control than tasting some water that you've just filtered?! That's what participants get to do in our program. Once they've built a system they also get to put their heart and soul into an artwork which is adhered to the system we donate on their behalf. It's a valuable opportunity to connect with the family that you're helping on the other side of the world. That family usually won't speak English but often there is an unspoken bond of gratitude forged when we explain that the people who sponsored this system designed this artwork for the family. For more information about the Water Works Program please visit www.waterworksprogram.com

We launched Water Work on April 25, 2015 and since that time have sponsored clean water for 500 households (about 5,000 people in total). The project is only just getting started but we've achieved some fantastic results and with the Water Works I only had to wait for 7 months before I could fly over and visit some of the beneficiaries of our charity project. For those readers who have never visited Africa I implore you to please do. It's an incredible part of the world and as a general rule you will be greeted with an overwhelming sense of love.

Recipients of Water Works Systems

During my first trip to Uganda in November, 2015 I visited with over 180 families as we gave out our water filtration systems and we even had cause to visit a local refugee camp. To put things into perspective the people at that refugee camp were not people trying to flee FROM Uganda, one of the poorest countries in the world; they were people fleeing TO Uganda. Not only was all of this overwhelming enough but I was also challenged by my own experience back in Australia. These people were not "detainees" as we would call them in Australia. These people were free to come and go as they pleased. There were no security guards, no fences. Just thousands of the poorest people on the planet who had been giving a relatively safe refuge, some land to farm (with no utilities) and access to a filthy creek running through the middle of the camp.

I will share a couple of stories about specific people I met in that refugee camp later in this book however I think it's fair to say that when you see people living in that kind of environment it's challenging. When you see that there are no sanitation systems in place in confronting. When you see those same people washing and drinking the same water that wild animals are drinking from it's frightening. When you see those same people laughing and smiling I'd have to say it's life-changing. It's patently unfair that I get to live in a four bedroom house with running water, power and the internet whereas those same smiling people fight for survival every day, yet maintain a positive attitude.

I think that global poverty, the very existence and the sheer scale of it, is one of the most challenging things to each of us in the Western world to come to terms with. We each do this in our own way. Some of us switch off when we see bad news on television. People like me just have trouble even imagining the way people live on the other side of the world. If we haven't seen it with our own two eyes then it doesn't happen. Some of us adopt ideology that pretends we were all born equal. Sadly, deep-down, I believe that we all know that our current circumstances in one way or another are due to sheer luck.

Over the last five years I've listened to a lot of people in the developing world share their stories. I've been privileged to be touched by the most inspiring people in the world and this book is my way of sharing some of the most touching of these stories. Each of the stories that I'm sharing is about people I've met during field trips as part of either the Helping Hands or Water Works programs. I feel privileged to be able to share these stories and hope that I do justice to their telling.

Chapter 2 – Key Insights

- The stories shared in this book are all derived from the authors experience within the Helping Hands and Water Works Programs.
- Both programs are philanthropic learning activities that result in life-changing gifts being provided to people in the developing world.
- The proceeds of this book will enable the continued operation and growth of both programs.

Chapter 3: Perspectives

I would like you to stop what you are doing and think of someone you care about. They could be anyone - maybe a work-colleague or family member. The only requirement is that you must genuinely care about that person. Now that you've got someone in mind I want you to begin to consider their context for a moment. Are they at work or are they studying? Are they married or single? Are there any major events in their life that you know about? Now I want you to dive a bit deeper. What are their hopes and fears? Have you ever seen them upset? If so, what triggered their emotion?

I want you to keep thinking about the person that we're reflecting on right now and ask the following questions:

(1) What are the things that they worry most about?

(2) What is the thing that you appreciate the most about them?

(3) Do they know how you feel about them?

(4) What do they think or feel about you?

If you do nothing else today I want you to find a way to let that person know how you feel about them. It wasn't the primary objective of this exercise but if we all took the time to tell the people we love what we feel about them more regularly I'm certain the world would be a better place.

Now… back to the primary objective of that exercise. The exercise we just went through was a conscious attempt to consider someone else's perspective. Hopefully as you went through each of those questions you felt an increasing capacity to empathise with the person in question. Maybe you even had new insights about that person that had never occurred to you before. You might have understood better what drives their behaviour under certain circumstances. Maybe you simply felt increased compassion and love for that person. Chances are, meditating on that other person's challenges took your mind off your own worries for a moment as well.

The concept of "Perspective" is a central theme of this book. We'd like you to think about a "Perspective" as a pair of glasses that you're looking at the world through. When we put on a set of glasses, it changes the way we see the world. Depending on the configuration of the lenses in our glasses, our view of the world is altered and it becomes difficult (almost impossible) to see the world in a different way without taking those glasses off our head again. We all have our own perspective which both enhances and distorts the way we see the world. We spend most of our lives wearing the same spectacles so we become VERY comfortable with them on. Often we are so comfortable with our perspectives that those little enhancements and distortions are invisible to us however they are still there.

Perspectives are powerful things. Not only do they prevent us from seeing the world as it is (without any bias or distortion) but a strong perspective also helps us focus in on some facts over others. Most of us would have heard of a self-fulfilling prophecy. This is where you hold a particular perspective so strongly that you not only are unwilling to challenge it, but you seek out data in the world that reinforces your perspective. With self-fulfilling prophecies those glasses keep on getting stronger the longer we look through them and in the long-term we find ourselves unable to see most of the data available out there in the world.

As we share various stories on coming pages we want you to consciously consider the perspectives of the people in each of those stories. Ask yourself what that person in question worries the most about; what you appreciate the most about them and ultimately what that person might think about you. It's a confronting exercise but we believe that each time you adopt another person's perspective, each time you take off your spectacles and put on somebody else's you're effectively collecting increasing amounts of data from the world and I believe that you can't help but make better decisions as a result.

The exercise of consciously taking on another person's perspective is an extremely valuable tool as a leader. The role of leadership is fundamentally one of influence. Effectively we all have the potential to be leaders; however the term only accurately applies to those of us that are able to influence others to think, feel or act in a different way. An effective leader is able to influence people, not just in the short-term but to influence long-term sustainable change. The greatest leaders don't always agree with everyone else but they are typically experts at understanding other people's perspectives. They know what drives those they are trying to influence and are able to make conscious decisions about whether or not to work with or challenge another person's perspective.

Can we ever truly change our perspectives?

The answer is "yes" but it's not always easy. Your perspective (or point of view) is a habit, just as strong as any other habit that you might be susceptible to. Our brains are much more sophisticated than many of us realise. They are constantly rewiring to enable efficient operation but once we establish a clear thinking pattern (or as I'd like to call it a habitual perspective) then our brain effectively hard-wires itself to enable that pattern and moves onto something else. The ability our brain has to hard-wire our thought patterns has actually been critical to our evolution. When we saw a bear or lion approaching, we didn't need to process things quickly, instantly we knew that we were in danger and could move onto more important variables (such as how to get out of the situation). Our ability to not continually reprocess information wasn't just critical during the time of the cave-man, that ability has helped us intellectually stretch to new heights in modern years as well. Speed-reading, touch-typing, mental arithmetic and driving all contain habitual perspectives that enable us to act without consciously thinking.

The problem with habitual perspectives is that sometimes they are inaccurate. Consider for a moment modern-day discrimination of people based on race, sexual orientation or gender. Usually those people who are discriminating against someone else aren't making a conscious choice to do so they just behave automatically. Maybe they are afraid due to ignorance. Maybe they were taught some inaccurate things as kids. Irrespective, those of us that discriminate against others are typically just implementing a habitual perspective. A thought pattern that is so ingrained in us that it doesn't even occur to us to challenge it. From an evolutionary perspective it makes sense – why tie up additional brain power on something that we know to be true? The problem is that often those habitual perspectives we hold turn out to be inaccurate and we don't often pause to challenge ourselves. Just like every habit, the more it's practiced, the stronger it becomes and the harder it is to change in the long-run.

A habitual perspective can be very similar to a learned behaviour. In fact, often it's those learned perspectives that drive the way we behave. However let's pause to think about our behavioural patterns. If you're a golfer, next time you're swinging a golf-club, try and stop yourself halfway through your swing. It's almost impossible unless you decided to do so in advance. Ever noticed which sleeve of your jacket you pull on first? If you put your right hand into you jacket first, try changing to the left and see how that feels? If you drive a car, think about the most common route that you drive along. Maybe it's a trip to work or home. Have you ever found yourself intending to drive somewhere else but when you've reached an intersection just automatically turning left when you should have gone straight or turned right? The habit of driving on that common route was so strong that your body made the choice for you and all of a sudden you were on the way to home, work or a friend's house even though you were intending to do something completely different.

The reality is that learned thought patterns are every bit as strong and habitual as physical learned behaviours and it's almost impossible to break them in the moment. We believe that the best way to help identify and shift inaccurate perspectives is to practice adopting someone else's. To do exactly what we did at the start of this chapter. Make a conscious decision to see the world through someone else's eyes. As a leader, taking the time to adopt a new perspective each day is a critical perspective. In fact, doing this can become a habit in itself and will become easier each time you practice it. Each time you practice adopting another perspective you're improving what scientists call your neural plasticity. Effectively, you're training your brain to be more agile, to be able to rewire itself more quickly.

Worried that adopting the perspective of others will leave you unclear about what your own perspective is? Don't concern yourself with this too much. Practicing taking on board other perspectives won't leave you without a perspective of your own. More likely, you'll end up with a very clear perspective on the world – it's just that your perspective is likely to be far more informed than it ever used to be.

One perspective we could all do without: Negative self-talk

The distorting impact of a false or inaccurate perspective can be powerfully illustrated by considering one perspective that many of us share. Negative self-talk. We all do it from time to time, replaying scenarios or events over and over in an attempt to try and solve some kind of problem or make ourselves feel better. It's called rumination and while everyone does it from time to time, some of us tend to ruminate more than others! The problem with rumination is that usually it makes us feel worse. People who ruminate more have also been shown to be more prone to depression and a range of other mental health issues.

Ruminative tendencies are not just isolated to a person's home or personal life, they also occur when you're at work. Anyone that has found themselves replaying a past meeting at work over and over again has experienced this. Rumination is definitely one of those habitual thought patterns that many of us share. It might start with you observing clear data - something irrefutable and unbiased. However, as you put on those 'worry wart' glasses and adopt that perspective, pretty soon you'll start interpreting that clear data in a very different way. Maybe you become convinced that you know what someone else was thinking. Perhaps you begin to see problems where there are none. Either way, you can almost feel it as this perspective starts to take hold and as you become increasingly convinced that everybody hates you, that you're a bad person and bad and your job and somehow something terrible is about to happen.

"So what?" I hear you ask. A number of recent studies out of the Australian National University (ANU) have begun to demonstrate that rumination significantly impairs our ability to solve complex problems at work. So not only does worrying too much make you see the world in a different way, it actually distorts your judgement as well, making you far less productive at work. If you're a real worrier, chances are that is just the beginning of another downward spiral. You begin worrying about the poor performance and predicting a similar outcome in the future. Sure enough, your worst fears are ultimately realised.

As a leader, or someone in a position of authority at work, home or socially, this insight can be a bit confronting because it is likely that you initiate other people's ruminative thoughts some of the time. How do you manage challenges as they arise? Do you have a well-structured conversation with your staff to get to the bottom of the issue, determine the appropriate course of action and move on or do you sometimes find yourself stuck ranting and raving about the same issue over and over again... sometimes days later? As leaders of people, we all have a responsibility to be aware of human nature and to use that knowledge to set up our people for success. Ranting and raving, prompting the people that we care the most about to begin a downward spiral of self-doubt and ultimately failure isn't something that any of us would set-out to do at the start of the day. However, that's precisely the impact that we can each have on people if we're not careful.

Of course having a degree of anxiety is helpful at times. If we never worried about anything, we would be unlikely to ever meet a deadline and would be prone to taking unnecessary risks. However, if the perspective that you habitually adopt is one of self-doubt, loathing or worrying about the past it's unlikely that you will ever reach your full potential. As a leader the challenge is even more pertinent. A leader must not only be aware of their own biases, they must practice understanding the perspective of those people that they seek to lead. Only then can a leader hope to truly engage with their people.

Metaphor as a unique form of perspective

By this point you should understand what a perspective is and how it can be both powerful and limiting. Actually every time we use a metaphor to describe a particular situation we are choosing to adopt a unique type of perspective. A metaphor is defined as a *"figure of speech in which a word or phrase is applied to an object or action to which it is not literally applicable"*. Although our day-to-day language is littered with metaphors, many of us haven't given these a second thought since school. In language, we use metaphors to help bring things to life, to illustrate more clearly what we are trying to communicate with one another. However, it is also true to say that when we incorporate a metaphor into the description of something, we are choosing to see things through a particular perspective.

Sometimes metaphors can be obvious and other times they can be more subtle. The idea of asking your colleagues to reconsider a large organisational change as just part of "the journey" is a relatively obvious (and common) metaphor that's used in the workplace. Asking employees to conceptualise a workplace initiative as a form of trip with a start, pathway and destination helps to illustrate that the change will not be instant, that there are requirements along the way, and there is a clear destination that is being worked towards even if that's not clear at the start of the journey. Another common metaphor that is often used in the workplace is a construction metaphor. If you've ever been asked to consider "getting the foundations right" before going any further or been presented with the "four pillars" or "building blocks" of a new idea in the workplace then you've been asked to do adopt a construction metaphor.

Other times, metaphors can be less obvious but equally powerful. The term "gene-mapping" is a cartographical metaphor that allows us lay-people to understand an extremely complicated scientific procedure. In recent years, the term "modelling" has been used frequently to describe scientific predictions. I would argue that this term is a form of metaphor that asks us to reimagine a scientific prediction as a form of prototype that's been moulded out of clay. It's not 100% accurate and might need to be changed down the track, but at this stage it's our best attempt. Once again, the metaphor is not obvious, but it's a form of figurative language that enables us to comprehend some very complicated mathematical procedures with a relatively childlike analogy.

Struggling to see how frequently we use metaphor in our daily lives? Each of the following statements includes a different type of metaphor (at times two different metaphors) to describe different elements of an organisational change. As you read through each of the below metaphors, consider first whether the use of that metaphor has helped you to understand the nature of the change. Secondly, consider any limitations that this metaphor has created for you.

- We need to think of this change differently. Sometimes the destination is less important than the journey.

- Our workplace is "littered" with ideas but we need to pick the best and stick with it.

- We are farming in really "fertile ground" here. Let's stick with it for a while.

- Although it might be hard now, we're creating something that's never existed before. We need to say goodbye to our past life and be reborn into this new way of doing things.

- Implementing this change will take some time. You can't turn a cruise-liner around a tight corner but you also wouldn't attempt to sail a tug-boat across the Pacific.

- We're building a "three legged stool" here – each element is critical.

- At this stage in our growth we need to focus on getting the foundations right.

- We've made ourselves a great cake here. Now we just need to add some icing and dust it with sprinkles.

- Our competitors are circling us and there's blood in the water.

We all have a preferred metaphor, just like we have a preferred perspective on many different issues in the workplace. What's important to understand is that each metaphor we use in the workplace can be equally enabling and limiting. Construction, cartographical, cooking and nautical metaphors will naturally prompt you to explore some completely different options and not others. Sometimes consciously choosing to change the metaphor can be an incredibly useful way of testing your own analysis of a situation. Have you been focussing too much on "the journey" and failed to realise that you're currently being "circled by sharks"?

So consciously choosing to change your preferred metaphor can be really powerful. However, being aware of your choice of metaphor is even more critical as a leader. You see, changing the metaphors we use when communicating critical workplace information will make your team look at a situation from a different perspective. Sometimes it won't make much of a difference. Other times your employees will identify new ideas or strategies that were previously unimaginable simply by changing the metaphor.

This book will profile a number of people that live in a very different context to you or me. Adopting their perspective is likely to prompt ideas in the workplace that you previously did not have. It's also likely to help you identify those things worth worrying about and those that are simply not worth it. After reading this book, my hope is that you will acquire a new, more accurate, view of what's important in the workplace (and world in general). In addition, my hope is that you will personally be empowered with the ability to help change the perspective of your team, workplace, family and friends.

Chapter 3 – Key Insights

- A perspective is a learned thinking pattern that is habitual.
- Practicing seeing things from other people's perspective promotes neuroplasticity and more accurate personal perspectives.
- Seeing things from other people's perspective is a critical habit for all leaders.
- Great leaders use metaphor consciously to ask their employees to see the world from a different perspective.

II.   CREATING AN INSPIRED CULTURE

This section of the book is dedicated to sharing stories that will inspire you to shape an inspired culture in your workplace. We start with the basics, explaining what culture is and how it can be sustainably shaped by good leaders that are not afraid of hard work. Then we introduce the concept of employee engagement, we explore the difference between happiness and engagement in the workplace and explore the difference between being motivated by fear or a genuine emotional attachment to the work.

Once we've explained what culture is and what we mean by employee engagement, we then explore seven characteristics which we believe could be transformative if authentically applied within your workplace. We call them the eight characteristics of an inspired culture and each of them are explored in turn:

1.   Purpose driven

2.   Community-based

3.   Truly collaborative

4.   Integrated work-life approach

5.   Innovative

6.   Holistic approach to value

7.   Sustainability

Each characteristic is illustrated by first exploring a story from the developing world. We ask that you open your heart to each story. Truly try and adopt each perspective that we share. Try it on for size and see the world through a different person's eyes. We believe that once you truly understand the messages within each of the stories in this section, you'll naturally find yourself considering ways to apply them back to your workplace, family or volunteer networks. Together, let's go out there and create an inspired culture in your workplace!

Chapter 4: The power of culture

The concept of "Africa Time"

Within minutes of arriving in Uganda I was introduced to the concept of "Africa Time". We all disembarked our plane and milled around waiting to go through customs in what had to be one of the slowest processes I had ever experienced. At the time I was travelling, Pope Francis was about to touch down in the country on his first ever visit to Uganda so I put the delay down to additional security procedures in anticipation of his visit. However, I was soon to realise that this was a much more engrained cultural norm than this. Many of the people I met in Uganda were amazing, intelligent, creative and loving people. It's just that they typically don't value time as much as we do in the west.

Each day that we would travel to the village to provide clean water systems to people, we would first visit with one of the local leaders within the community before travelling onto our end destination. Each day we would drop in, spend some time with the family, then go on to meet with the new water recipients for the day. Following the distribution exercise we would then travel back to that same leader's residence and share a meal with his family before moving on for the night.

The process was lovely and really promoted a sense of togetherness that stayed with us throughout the day. It was really nice and I could see how it was a productive thing for us to do as a distribution team. The morning meeting was a chance for last minute preparations and agreements and the afternoon meeting was an opportunity for a debrief and wind-down. It wasn't until the final day when I realised that there was a deeper cultural expectation involved.

On the final day of distributions we were in a bit of a rush. We had our transportation waiting to pick us up in a neighbouring township. He was there already waiting but we were 2 hours' drive away. You can only imagine that if you had a taxi driver waiting for you with the meter running in the developed world that not only would you be in a rush, but your hosts would also understand the problem and be in a rush as well. That was not the case in Uganda. On that last day I realised for the first time that visiting with the leader's family and sharing a meal with them was not just a productive thing to do it was a cultural expectation. Not only would it bring shame on his family if he did not share a meal with us, but we would be seen as terribly rude if we did not accept his hospitality.

People doing aid-work in Uganda have a saying "TIA (This Is Africa)". It's a reminder that the culture here is very different to back home. Start-times are always flexible. People often will not show up until they see you there then they materialise from nowhere. Formal community meetings often go ALL DAY LONG but people arrive at different times then stay for a long time once they do arrive. It's fair to say that "Africa Time" really frustrates me. However, it's also fair to say that I can see some real benefits in being able to ignore the time and truly give your undivided attention to the people you love and or care about in the moment.

We don't do it consciously but I believe in Western cultures we tend to take pride in how "busy" our schedules are. We don't necessarily expect people to be rushing about 24 hours a day but we do seem to want people be driven, goal-oriented and actively working towards something... anything will do. People who don't have full schedules tend to be frowned upon and there's a well-known management technique which says "If you want to get something done then give it to a busy person". I know that statement off by heart because I know it's one of my favourite sayings. However, the implication of that saying is that busy people find a way to "get stuff done" and those people who aren't busy are generally slackers. We definitely worship at the altar of "being busy" over here but if I'm to compare that general approach to what I experienced in Uganda it couldn't be more different. I think it's fair to say that sometimes "Africa Time" is not always helpful but the same could be said about western approaches as well.

Incredible India

Another extremely unique and beautiful culture that I've had exposure to as part of the Helping Hands project is India. Of course I wouldn't be naïve enough to suggest that there is simply one culture throughout the entire country of India. It's such a diverse, incredible and huge place that there are many cultures co-existing in that country. My cultural observations about this amazing country are based on my limited experience there.

In the western world we nod our head up and down to communicate agreement and shake our head left to right to indicate disagreement. Within India, both nodding and shaking of the head are relatively uncommon. Instead, people will often tilt there head from side to side as they are listening or talking with you. When you ask the local people what this means the common answer is "sometimes it means yes, sometimes it means no, sometimes it means maybe." To this day I've got incredibly positive memories of interacting with people in India and I believe that at least in part the "head wobble" as I call it is part of an intention to avoid offending someone else at all costs. I think it's purposely ambiguous but comes from a place of deep respect for others.

A hand recipient in India

Another observation from Helping Hands fitting events attended in India was the high degree of formality in many interactions. A number of dignitaries are invited to speak at each event and all of the people involved in our projects will typically go out of their way to meet each other, shake their hand, introduce themselves formally and also find out about each other. Perhaps this cultural norm is in part motivated by a relatively stratified society (some would call it a "class system") but irrespective of the cause of this cultural norm it just seems to work over there. That high degree of formality during introductions and the launch of different events truly does promote mutual respect and dignity for all people involved and I found it really nice. Within India there is also plenty of formality in the paperwork and processes you are asked to follow for even the most mundane of tasks. If in Australia or the USA you tried to force people through the kinds of processes that are common-place in India you would have people complaining and refusing to adhere to the rules, but over there people show an incredible amount of restraint.

I'm not pretending for a second that I've accurately described two whole cultures in just a few paragraphs. That would not be possible. However I've attempted to share a small window into a few cultural norms within the countries I've visited.

Culture is best described as "the way things are done around here". It is typically made up of a range of cultural norms that everyone adheres to - best described as behavioural expectations. Moving their head courteously when discussing something important is clearly a cultural norm in some parts of India. It's the way you're expected to behave. If we all moved to Uganda tomorrow, you would relatively quickly realise the significance of "sharing a meal" with friends and leaders within the community. It's more than a friendly gesture, it's a cultural norm. If you don't adhere to that cultural norm you will quickly cause offence and frustration for others.

Creating an Inspired Culture in your workplace.

Organisational culture is essentially the same as the regional cultures that I've been describing. Every company has its own social norms and rules that define "the way we do things around here". Just like it would be ignorant and ill-informed to say that one country's culture is better than another, workplace cultures are different in every company and there is no one "correct" culture. Having said that, you can relatively quickly determine whether a workplace culture is productive or otherwise by asking three simple questions:

- Does this company's culture enable successful implementation of the company vision and strategy?

- Does the company's culture create an engaged workforce?

- Does the company' culture benefit the society it operates in?

If a workplace culture impedes the company's ability to implement its strategy and vision then clearly that culture is unsustainable. If the existing culture within a company is 100% aligned to the company strategy but results in a disengaged workforce then that culture is also unsustainable. In the short-term a disengaged workforce that is motivated by fear or survival instincts might be able to deliver the outcomes required, but it's simply not sustainable in the long-run.

We believe that every company should aspire to create an "Inspired Culture". Employees that are part of an inspired culture take the success or failure of their company personally. When they finish a day's work they can't help but talk about it with friends and family because they are so proud of what they are achieving together. Inspired cultures don't go out there to beat their competitor, that's a happy byproduct, but it's not their primary goal. Inspired cultures also create enormous value for their shareholders, stakeholders and communities even though that might not be their primary goal.

Although the characteristics of each inspired culture are unique to that workplace, we believe that there is one factor which they all have in common. Within an inspired culture, each and every employee feels satisfied that they are fulfilling their destiny at the company. In an inspired culture, we believe each and every employee is able to believe that their contribution is helping them achieve (sometimes in a very small way) what they were put on the planet to do. Effectively there is a profound alignment between the purpose of the company and each individual's sense of personal purpose or calling.

Cultural Change

Workplace culture is notoriously difficult to change. In many ways, the resilience of workplace culture could be likened to regional culture. Although we could all point to some changes in our national identity and culture over the last decade or so, typically cultural change is a slow, evolutionary process. It takes time and during the process we don't even notice it happening. It might just be upon reflection and retrospective consideration that we even notice something has changed. The problem with this is the workplace culture is one of the single most important variables that lead towards organisational success in a modern economy.

There are a range of situations where workplace leaders seek rapid cultural change or cannot afford for the process to take many years. As a result of this, the consulting industry has seen an explosion of boutique consultancies each promising to help navigate and accelerate the difficult process of cultural change within the workplace. Typically those consultancies (and their projects) fail to meet the lofty goals they set for themselves. In my experience, that is normally because they have failed to acknowledge cultural change as a battle that needs to be waged on multiple fronts. You can't just invest in an employee survey, some focus groups and then hope for the best. Much of the work required is not "sexy" by any measure... it's a tough grind, but its 100% necessary if you are to deliver sustainable cultural change.

In our own experience we've found that in order for a cultural change initiative to be sustainable it needs to work on four different levels (often simultaneously):

- Perspectives: We need to change the way that employees see the company and the way that they feel about it.

- Systems: Workplace IT systems, policies and processes all shape the behaviour of employees and these must be realigned to the new cultural objectives of the firm.

- Role-modelling: Key workplace leaders (key influencers as well as people in management positions) must role-model the behaviours that are expected moving forward.

- Measurement: Robust measures must be implemented to evaluate progress over time. Such measures should be utilised repeatedly as change program progresses.

Shifting Employee Perspectives...

First of all, if an "inspired culture" is at its core, an emotional attachment to the workplace. It's a deeply personal thing. For many of us it's hard to talk about feelings and it's even harder still to change those feelings via analysis. That's why we believe that the start of every journey towards an inspired culture requires an experience that is so powerful that it jolts us out of our current way of viewing the world. This is normally accomplished with the help of either the Helping Hands Program (www.helpinghandsprogram.com.au) or Water Works Program (www.waterworksprogram.com). These programs are much more than just an opportunity to do some charity work. They are an opportunity to re-connect with our inner child; that inner child that used to dream naïvely about changing the world. The programs reminds us what it feels like to be engaged in 100% purpose-driven work and in doing so creates an opportunity to reconnect with the vision, mission and values of the companies that we work for.

Realigning Workplace Systems…

No training program, irrespective of how powerful it is, will create lasting employee engagement in just a few hours. One thing it can do is get employees to see the world from a different perspective and in doing so create the momentum and space for change. However, following the training experience, if those employees go back to the workplace and are forced through the same old processes that are preventing an inspired culture to begin with then it's only a matter of time before employee engagement becomes just an aspiration again. We believe that sustainable cultural change requires objective evaluation of all systems and processes. An experienced cultural change consultant will often have benchmark policies available however this exercise isn't just about doing a policy benchmarking exercise or using a "cookie cutter" approach. To truly create an inspired culture you need to be honest as a business about which specific system is preventing the kind of behaviours that you want to see from team and have the courage to make a change. This can be much harder than we think as often the systems that need to be changed are the most engrained processes in the workplace. That's no accident – your current culture is also engrained and if key leaders are not willing to change some of those most established processes then in our experience your workplace is not serious about cultural change.

Role-modelling Behaviour…

This element of creating an inspired culture is the easiest to describe, but often the most difficult to implement. Employees will often take even the subtlest of clues from their leaders as encouragement to behave in a particular way. If a leader is particularly well-respected, employees will watch that person very carefully and do their best to emulate what they are seeing. To embed an inspired culture, the leaders in your organisation MUST role-model the behaviours that you believe are important.

Research into leadership is one of the most fraught areas of workplace research. Each new book that comes out launches a new buzz-word or leadership model and the books that are written are almost always in advance of any sound research. Of course most workplaces will define what they believe "leadership" is in their company. They will typically also have a leadership development program in place to train the skills and knowledge required. Our suggestion is not to be too distracted by the latest piece of leadership research when you're involved in cultural change. Instead, simply work to identify who are the influencers in your organisation (either via the position they hold or the sway they have with their peers). Once you've identified those key influencers, you need to work closely with them to teach the kinds of behaviours you are looking to promote in the workforce. Describe those behaviours inside and out: What do they look like? How do they differ in different circumstances? What do they NOT look like? Under pressure, if they are finding it difficult to demonstrate appropriate behaviours what should they do?

Measuring success…

In our experience cultural change must be seen as an iterative process. What we mean is that it's very rare that you will embark on a change of this magnitude, have a beginning and an end, then implement a linear plan that goes about achieving success. We think that a much more realistic option is to think about cultural change as a cyclical process where you continually need to check in throughout the process and realign your intervention. Of course you should always embark on the process with the expectation that you're going to need to invest in some initiatives across each of the 4 key areas we've described (perspectives, systems, role-modelling and measurement) but it's also critical to have a degree of agility throughout the process. If you put in place the correct measurement and evaluation systems at the start of the change you will not only be able to track your success over time, you'll also be intervene before it's too late if one of your planned interventions is not working or having an undesired impact.

Spotlight on symbols

One thing that we often notice when embarking on cultural change work with our workplace clients is that often certain systems, leadership behaviours and KPIs can take on a "symbolic" status within the organisation. What we mean by that is that the thing in question takes on a life of its and is held up as evidence by employees of what is wrong, right or indifferent about the organisation. One of the most important things a company can do when embarking on cultural change is to conduct a "symbols audit" to identify which of those things in the workplace have gained symbolic status as it's typically by consciously choosing to maintain or challenge those symbols that a change agent can have the greatest impact.

Allow me to explain further the power of symbols by sharing a story about my recent experience with Apple (the company). Although, I was interacting with them as a customer (not consultant), I was blown away by some of the organisational processes and symbols that they had in place. The rest of this article both describes my experience, as well as identifies some lessons that we can all learn about more effective use of symbols in shaping organisational culture.

I had never dealt with Apple before purchasing my current iPhone. As such, I was completely unprepared for the experience that I recently had when I went into their main store in George St, Sydney to get my phone fixed.

When I got to the Apple store at 7:30am there was already a line-up of 6 people waiting for the shop to open. I assumed that they were lining up with faults (just like me) but was a little shocked to discover that they were all lining up to purchase products. I felt a little queasy to be honest, as I stood there overhearing excited stories about Apple products from converted disciples of the company.

I started looking around, in an attempt to avoid eye contact with the Apple fanatic / cyclist (still wearing his helmet) standing in the queue next to me. That's when I noticed muffled clapping and could vaguely make out a group of employees (all in red shirts) standing in a circle inside the building. They were obviously having a pre-start meeting but it sounded more like a pep rally.

Shortly thereafter, one of the staff came outside the locked doors to talk to each of the people in the line to check what we were here for and give us advice about what to do once the store opened. I couldn't believe that they have so many people lining up before they open that they need a standard process to deal with it! After working his way through the line, the staff member in the red shirt (and board shorts) gave me advice on what to do once I entered the store. Although I didn't understand what he was saying at first (due to some jargon), I eventually figured out that all he was saying was that I needed to speak to someone with a red shirt on (in other words speak to practically anyone and they will be able to help you).

At this stage it was already clear that this company was a bit different, but then the doors opened....

What's so interesting about that? Well, there wasn't an old, disgruntled employee with a tired and mildly irritated look on their face opening the door. Instead, there were three people, all with smiles on their faces and together they opened the three bi-fold doors simultaneously, in a clearly pre-prepared, almost theatrical manner. At the same time all the other staff (who by this stage were stationed throughout the store) began to cheer, whistle and clap! By the time I walked into the store I was so disoriented I had completely forgotten to be mildly irritated about my broken telephone!

Sure enough, I went to the first person with a red shirt and she was able to help me. She booked me in for an appointment and then I went upstairs to find a technician. There was literally 50 or 60 staff standing around so I had no trouble finding the right place. I sat down to wait for my technician then was greeted by name (not sure how they did that) and asked to come up to the counter. I immediately sat down and started to talk about my problem... only to look up and see that the young guy was holding his hand out and smiling to introduce himself. After we had shaken hands I told him my problem and within 30 seconds he informed me "Matt we need to give you a new phone. Have you backed up your data?"... "Yep" was my response. "That's great... just wait right there". 2 minutes later and I had been given my new phone, signed a 1-page form, had shaken my technician's hand again and was walking out the front of the store with a brand spanking new phone!

The purpose of this example is not to give a free advertisement for Apple or the iPhone (I have a feeling that they are doing pretty well without my help). The reason I felt compelled to write about it was because I had never come across a company before that utilises symbols so well! A symbol to me is something highly sensory – often visual - that communicates what a company values in the workplace. Symbols are particularly important in business because they have the potential to shape an organisations culture much more than many other decisions or actions that a manager might take. Let's list some of the most obvious symbols that I noticed at Apple:

- Everyone wore red t-shirts and mismatched pants (ranging from board shorts to jeans). This symbolised to me that the company is young; they value individualism, and of course are a bit cool.

- The young man coming out to greet us before the doors opened symbolised to me that the company cared and appreciated that I was waiting.
- The door being opened simultaneously by three guys was a bit weird. However, it did demonstrate how they were a company that had considered the customer experience very carefully; down to the finest detail.
- The cheering as we all walked in really did not feel very Australian. I felt a bit like I was walking into an American-style pep rally. However, who could escape the key message... We want your visit to our store to be an exciting event and we are all excited to see you!
- The deliberate attempt to shake my hand showed me that this was a technician that cared about the people side of the problem.
- Even the fact that the 1-page form I signed was written in plain English and was no more than 100-200 words. There were no catches, no fine

print, and no tricks! At no stage did someone try and hint that maybe this was my fault.

I could probably go on and on about my experience with Apple. However, like I said, this isn't meant to be an advertisement for Apple. The point is that this is a company that, without words, communicated to me that it was different. They appeared to care about my situation even before they were open for business, and once they did open, they exceeded all of my expectations in terms of the simplicity and speed of the process.

Now think about the cultural change that you would like to make in your workplace. Are there any simple symbolic actions you could take that could make all the difference? Symbols take on a special status in any cultural change exercise because they are important to consider throughout all elements of your change journey (not just systemic change). I can assure you that if you identify and implement the appropriate symbolic changes early in your cultural change journey; chances are you will have made a giant stride in the right direction of creating an inspired culture.

Chapter 4 – Key Insights

- Culture is a powerful tool both globally and within the workplace.
- If you want to shape a sustainable "Inspired Culture" in your workplace then you need to work on 4 different levels: challenge existing perspectives, realign organisational systems, role-model different behaviours and put in place measurement systems to evaluate your progress over time.
- Consider "Symbols" within the workplace as a critical tool that reinforces or challenges your workplace culture.

Chapter 5: Happiness and engagement

In November of 2015 I was lucky enough to travel to Uganda for the first time. Specifically, we had accumulated enough Water Works sponsorships to provide clean water to our first entire village in Uganda. That's the way our program works, we want to bring communities together, not force them apart. So we avoid doing anything that will create jealousy or potential crime by giving one family a water filtration system and not another. We simply wait a tiny bit longer until we have enough water systems to provide every single household, school and health centre in the same village. We want to make a really big impact in a small area each time we visit a village and so that's what we try and do.

Travelling into a foreign land is always an experience but I must say that travelling into the small village of Katoma was unlike anything I had experienced before. The village was a 1.5 hour drive away from the nearest town via a dirt road. It was also 1.5 hours away from water, electricity, sewerage, mobile phone reception or any other utilities that you might expect in today's day and age. The land at Katoma is incredibly fertile and lush. Fruit trees and green crops are abundant with mud-huts being the typical accommodation. The entire scene was beautiful and incredibly photogenic. Sadly, this beautiful scenery was also juxtaposed by people obviously living in extreme poverty. Some children owning only one set of clothes, and people carrying large yellow jerry-cans full of water that had been retrieved from various untreated and dangerous water sources around the village.

As my first trip into this part of the world I was obviously a bit speechless at what I saw but also excited to make a difference and we went straight to the location of our first water distribution efforts. Immediately we were met by what felt like an army of small smiling children who swamped us without delay with the biggest smiles one could ever hope for. Any thoughts of sympathy were buried amidst the unbelievable joy that I felt at being so well received by all of these smiling children. The process of distributing water filtration systems and training the recipients on their use took four days and at the end of that time 180 families now had a brand new water system that would eliminate any water borne diseases from their water supply. Every day was similar. We would be greeted by some of the friendliest and happiest beautiful people in the world and each day I would return to our 1-star hotel feel exhausted but incredibly satisfied.

On the third night, we had cause to visit a refugee settlement camp. It was probably one of the single most moving experiences of my life. On the way to that camp I was quite apprehensive. This was my first visit to a refugee camp and based on news reports back home this was exactly the kind of place that assault, rape and riots are common-place. At least that was the story that is painted by the media in Australia. I was a little scared but putting on a brave face. Beyond my fear of the unknown I also had nagging doubts about how we would be received at the camp. Katoma, I told myself, was a different place altogether, we were foreigners but we were foreigners who were bearing some pretty incredible gifts and it made sense that people would be delighted to see us. At the refugee camp I wasn't bearing any gifts, they were not on my list to receive water systems during this trip and I was quite worried that our reception would be less warm as a result.

My fears (and my perspective) turned out to be completely unfounded. Once we got to our destination all of the kids once again were incredibly happy and it was easy to get lost taking photos and showing them the way the camera worked. They loved seeing the camera. For most of the kids it was the first time they had seen a digital camera which meant it was also the first time they had seen their own beautiful faces in a photo. The photos don't even do justice to how beautiful and happy these kids looked. The camp has thousands of people living there and the majority of them were children, sadly in this part of the world I'm told that a large number of these children were likely AIDS orphans. Truly, I couldn't imagine more tragic circumstances under which to meet someone but once again everywhere I looked there were smiling, happy faces.

Still at the refugee camp, as I played with the children I heard some music coming from close-by and walked around the back of a church building to find a group of kids practicing a song and dance. Once again these were beautiful, happy kids. It was a sight unlike any that I had ever seen before and I recorded a video. They sang two different songs and our translator told us that they were singing in multiple languages. The children all came from different countries and it was an honour to witness their beautiful singing and choreographed dance-moves. I'm told that the first song was actually a welcome song for me. I didn't realise it but the children changed the song they were singing as soon as they saw me come around the corner.

The words to the second song were "Our God loves us and we will harvest the good things in our land. We have nothing but we have everything because of our God." It still brings tears to my eyes as I think about the words to that song and their striking truth. Many of those children were orphans. Not only did they have few, if any, material possessions, but they didn't even have a mother and father.

Happy Kids

The truth is that many of us don't take accountability for our own emotions. We extend blame for the way we are feeling on the others and on the context in which we find ourselves. "Once I get through this big project I'll have the time to be happy again" we tell ourselves. The truth is, the biggest things many of us worry about in the developed world are positively ridiculous when you put them in the context of this story. Job security, office politics, traffic, a rude email from a loved one simply don't compare to the plight of a child living without parents, clean water, sanitation or a change of clothes.

Truly, if the children I met were happy then it MUST be that our emotions have nothing to do with the context we find ourselves in. Happiness is a choice and if you're reading this book, chances are you've won the genetic lottery. You live in a country with clean water, electricity and a welfare system. If you ever find yourself struggling to manage your emotions, please think about the kids we met in that refugee camp back in 2015.

Happiness versus engagement

We live in a society that seems obsessed with the pursuit of happiness. If you're not happy every moment of every day then we're told that it's not normal and there must be something wrong with us. Our consumerist attitude seems to have translated into more than just an attitude towards shopping and become a way of life. It wasn't that long ago that happiness was seen as a temporary emotional state and longer term concepts such as contentment and satisfaction were more highly valued.

Of course employees can be happy at work too. The emotion is no different irrespective of the context. Once again, if you're seeking "happy" employees at all times, there's a risk that you are fighting our very biology. Happiness is a short-term emotion that is rarely lasting. I think of employee engagement as a broader concept than happiness. True workplace engagement is an emotional attachment to the company and/or the work you are doing. It's a deeply personal construct that reflects the way an employee sees themself and identifies as a person. If I'm truly engaged in my work, the success of my company feels like my success, I take the output of my work seriously and I exert discretionary effort, not because I have to, but because I want to; in fact I almost can't stop myself.

There is no silver-bullet to creating an engaged workforce and we know that extraneous variables like pay and conditions have little or nothing to do with it. Employee engagement is a deeply personal construct and in our experience this is related to three primary variables:

- The extent to which an employee feels like they are able to live their life's *purpose* with your company. Not only is it important that the employee understands and believes in the underlying purpose of your business, they need to feel as though that purpose is aligned with their own.

- The extent to which each employee feels like they are able to *grow* as a person. Employees need to feel stretched and challenged and feel as though they are growing their skills, knowledge and experience. We all know what it feels likes to feel as though we are stagnating in a job. Employees are looking for more than just fulfilling a job description and being comfortable. To really take their engagement to the next level you need to help them become better people and feel as though they are moving forward with their lives.
- Finally, the extent to which employees feel as though they are *empowered* in their roles. Very few of us enjoy being told what to do and having someone watch over our shoulder as we go about following those instructions. It doesn't matter how junior or small the role is, there is always an opportunity to give your employees some ability to self-direct their work and make some decisions for themselves. In fact, if you try and proceduralise out all discretion from a person's work you'll quickly realise that you can't possibly design for every possible scenario. Employers need to empower their people if they want them to perform at their best.

Of course there are only three key ingredients to employee engagement but that doesn't mean it's easy to create that kind of environment for every employee. I am the first person to admit that at times I'm a positively terrible leader and I break every rule that I espouse. I know how difficult this stuff is. That doesn't mean that it's any less correct. Truly, there is no short-cut to employee engagement. It involves leaders fostering deep personal relationships with their staff and helping craft the dream job for each and every employee that works for them.

Fear: engagement's ugly cousin

It would be remiss of us to talk about that refugee camp without admitting that these are people who are fighting for survival. Many of the kids I've met are orphans attempting to carve out a new life in a foreign land, sometimes without even speaking the local language. It's scary stuff on so many different levels. My understanding about the refugee settlement camp we visited is that when people are settled there they are provided with very little. As far as I could tell, the people were even required to build their own accommodation and collect water from a truly filthy water source that ran through the entire camp. The only things those people are given as far as I could tell was free access to acres upon acres of maize fields from which they were free to farm and collect food.

That situation probably sounds positively inhumane as you read my description. How could we possibly not treat asylum seekers in a more generous way? No accommodation or utilities? The truth is that you can't interpret the generosity of this refugee camp correctly without considering it from a Ugandan perspective. You see the villagers that we work with in Uganda all build their own mud-hut houses as well. Generally the people we work with in Africa are subsistence farmers who primarily eat what they are able to grow in their own backyard. They then trade for any other wares that they need using a barter system. So when you consider what asylum seekers are given within that refugee settlement camp, they are actually provided with exactly the same resources that many local Ugandans have. As tough as it might sound, building your own accommodation is a normal expectation. So what do people do when they first move in and don't have a home of their own? As confronting as this sounds, the sense of community in Uganda is much stronger than it is in Western cultures. I can almost guarantee that each of those people would be the recipients of extraordinary generosity from other community members. Often it's the people that have the least in life that are the most generous with what they have.

Truly engaged employees don't work because they are frightened or fighting for their existence. Engaged employees aren't working because they have to do so to survive. An engaged workforce genuinely feels a sense of affection for their workplace, they buy-in to the purpose of the business and care about the output of their work because of that. It appears obvious that this is the state we should all strive for but in my experience, so many of us are working harder because of a sense of fear. Fear of losing their job, of being belittled by coworkers or some other work-related stressor.

On face value, the work output of both people, in the short-term at least, will look similar. However, it's not sustainable and there are biological reasons why this is so. One of our most fundamental instincts is to run or fight for our survival when we feel threatened. It's an instinct that is hardwired into our anatomy. When we become aware of a threat, our body automatically and simultaneously triggers a range of physiological responses via our sympathetical nervous system. Just some of the physical responses triggered include (source: http://en.wikipedia.org/wiki/Fight-or-flight_response):

- Acceleration of heart and lung action
- Paling or flushing, or alternating between both
- Inhibition of stomach and upper-intestinal action to the point where digestion slows down or stops
- General effect on the sphincters of the body
- Constriction of blood vessels in many parts of the body
- Liberation of nutrients (particularly fat and glucose) for muscular action
- Dilation of blood vessels for muscles
- Inhibition of the lacrimal gland (responsible for tear production) and salivation
- Dilation of pupil (mydriasis)
- Relaxation of bladder
- Inhibition of sexual arousal
- Auditory exclusion (loss of hearing)
- Tunnel vision (loss of peripheral vision)
- Acceleration of instantaneous reflexes
- Shaking

These physiological responses all work together to ensure that we are ideally prepared for violent physical action at short notice. When you think about it our bodies are truly amazing things!

During my Christmas holidays a couple of years ago I was out fishing on my kayak and experienced the fight or flight response first hand. Things were going well and I had caught my first fish quickly. Even better still, I had the whole beach to myself and I was on top of the world! However, things changed when I caught my second fish. I was reeling it in and got it to within 2 metres of the boat when along came a large Hammerhead shark which ate my approximately 40cm fish, together with my 10cm lure, whole. It came and went within 2 seconds and the whole incident was so quick that I didn't have time to think.

Initially, I was surprised at how composed I was. Panicking in the middle of the ocean, with no-one else around except for hungry sharks would not have been the best idea and I was proud that I had not done so. Although scared, I began to tie a new lure onto my line. The only problem was that I was incapable of performing such fine dexterous movements, thanks to my flight or fight instincts, and I promptly dropped my rod into the water. Ten minutes later, after struggling to retrieve my fishing gear, I was overcome with exhaustion and suddenly felt very sick. I was no longer scared of the shark at this stage, but I could physically feel all the adrenaline in my system. My body wanted me to run and I wasn't letting it. Instead I did the next best thing and paddled to shore.

Although you could argue that in this instance my basic instincts to get out of there were correct, on one level, they also let me down and potentially got me into an even more perilous situation (attempting to retrieve an overboard fishing rod).

How often do our most basic, flight or fight instincts let us down at work?

When we go to work to do our jobs, we do not leave our sympathetic nervous systems behind and we can often experience similar difficulties to what I experienced while trying to tie my line. Even though most of us do not experience life-threatening situations at work, many people do feel threatened at work. Feelings are unique, personal things and the situations that make people feel threatened at work will differ greatly from person to person. Maybe it's an argument with a colleague. Maybe it's speaking up at a meeting or public speaking. Maybe it's something as simple as a supervisor watching you work over your shoulder. The things that make each of us feel threatened are different but when we do, we are likely to experience many of the physiological responses mentioned above. The problem with this is that, unless you're a professional boxer, or one of those guys on the Deadliest Catch TV program, the fight or flight response is not going to be particularly useful. Here are some simple examples of when the fight or flight response can actually prevent us from doing our best at work:

- Reacting aggressively (and inappropriately) to colleagues at work
- Attempting to write or type with shaky hands and an increased heart-rate
- Experiencing difficulty listening to others
- Feeling burnt out or exhausted after a big meeting or difficult discussion

So... as amazing as our bodies are they do not always serve us well in the workplace. This doesn't mean that we need to be victims of our fight or flight response!

Here are some tips about how to conquer the fight or flight response:

- Be honest with yourself and be prepared to admit when you feel threatened
- Identify any trends and patterns. What normally makes you feel this way and how do you typically react?
- Identify the early warning signs. Do you start to feel hot or sweaty or are there other unique symptoms?
- Identify any inappropriate behavioural response patterns
- Practice delaying those predictable behavioural responses when you notice your early warning signs. Try delaying the behaviour for a little while at first and gradually increase this delay over time.
- Once you are able to delay some of those inappropriate behavioural responses, you will find it much easier to change the behavioural responses and learn a new, more productive habit
- Identify common inappropriate fears or feelings
- Systematically challenge these fears or feelings and gain professional help if required
- Share your struggle with a trusted colleague or your manager. You colleagues

cannot support you if they are not aware of the challenges that you are confronting (eg. if you are afraid of public speaking, why not get some training and do a bit more practice?)

Of course challenging one's fears and modifying ingrained behaviour can often be a long and difficult journey. As such, most people will need help from a friend, family member, psychologist or workplace coach to assist with their journey. However, as with most long-term journeys the first step is often the hardest one.

We all experience the fight or flight response at times. It's something we are biologically programmed to experience and nothing to be embarrassed about. Having said that, if you are a leader who wants to lead an inspired workforce, choose engagement over fear any day of the week. Sure, from time to time engaged employees make mistakes, but they will improve and keep coming back time and time again. Truly, while the fight for survival is an entirely appropriate motivator in the refugee camp, it has no place in a modern workplace.

Chapter 5 – Key Insights

- Happiness is a choice and can exist and thrive in the most horrendous of circumstances
- You cannot motivate an employee through pay alone. Once you've met someone's most basic needs, true motivation comes from a different place than that.
- Employee engagement is an emotional attachment to the workplace.
- There is no short-cut to creating employee engagement. It requires enabling each employee to:
  - o Fulfil their personal sense of **purpose** at work
  - o **Grow** as a person
  - o Be **empowered** to make decisions
- Motivating employees through fear and survival is unproductive and likely to prompt uncharacteristic errors.

Chapter 6: The power of purpose

Within either Asia or Africa, the average distance walked to collect water is 6 kilometres (just under 3 miles). If you're walking at an average pace that's a solid 1 hour walk and for half of that time you'll be carrying, pulling or pushing several litres of water. At the villages I've visiting typically water is collected either early in the morning or at dusk. The reason for this is to avoid the heat of the middle of the day. Often this chore is delegated to children who take the job very seriously. They don't have a choice.

It's important to understand the long distances that many people walk just to collect water. Of course that concept is so foreign to many of us. We turn on the tap and have an unlimited, healthy supply, however in many parts of the world this is something that the family needs to plan for each day. Each household needs to plan their water collection activities sufficiently to ensure that they have a minimum of 5 Litres per day per person but the average consumption is 10 Litres so most families would plan for that level of consumption. If I've got a household of 10 people I need to haul 100 Litres back to my home every single day and each trip will take on average 1 hour. The distance, volume and time involved is often the motivator of some extremely inventive approaches. Many people have bicycles that are almost dedicated to water collection. They strap ropes and other attachments to the bicycles to enable them to carry several jerry-cans of water at any given time. By the time they have loaded up the bicycle with water containers it's not possible to ride the bike anymore but they can still push it along the road. Presumably the breaks on the bike are useful when pushing a huge volume of weight along on the bikes.

Another critical daily chore in many such communities is wood collecting. Each household (assuming 10 members of the household) will likely use about 10 cubic metres of wood each year. That's roughly 5 Tonnes per year (11,000 pounds). Based on those assumptions, each family needs to gather about 13 kilograms of wood per day (30 pounds). If they fail in this task then it's a significant inconvenience. Without electricity or gas-powered stoves, fire is critical for cooking. Many families use a coal fire stove which is simply a collection of stones on the ground put together carefully to ensure that no hot-coals escape. A fire is then lit in the stove and coals are heated up, a cast iron pot is then used to cook almost everything in the kitchen. Once again, necessity is the mother of all invention. People in the developing world are able to do an awful lot with very little. If a family is lucky enough to have a separate kitchen area there will be no running water, no benchtops, no range-hood and no electricity. Just a number of containers to store things and if they need bench space a clean cloth will be spread out on the ground either inside the kitchen or outside.

Obviously wood and water collection are simple, basic necessities. However, if the family also owns any life-stock or animals such as chickens then these creatures might need some tending. If the family is to eat meat that day then the animals must be slaughtered and cleaned in time for the meal. Perhaps crops or fruit-trees might also need to be tended to. Potentially the meal that the family is planning on eating might require some processing. If you require flour (or similar) then you'll need to grind the materials yourself. If you have some money and would like to purchase these goods (or trade them) at a local market then you might need to walk for several kilometres to execute this task as well.

I think it's fair to say that living in a remote village with no access to town utilities is a difficult job and everyone needs to lend a hand. Unsurprisingly though, all of this just happens without a fuss. Parents and children both understand that without completing their daily chores the family's health and wellbeing will be put at risk. The family might even make a conscious decision to do more chores than required in case of a storm or opportunity to show hospitality to a neighbour. Once again, such chores get done with a limited amount of fuss.

I remember being about 11 when my parents first tried to give me a few chores so I could earn my pocket money (i.e. allowance). The idea was of course for me to lend a hand around the house by taking on a small job or two and as a result earn some token spending money. It was a good idea in practice and certainly seemed to work on television but I was a real brat. I don't particularly remember getting a lot of pocket money but I equally don't remember doing any chores. Normally I would get by doing the bare minimum and everything would then change if my parents got upset with me... typically after that a flurry of activity ensued.

One great example that demonstrates my typical behaviour was what happened on "cleaning day". We were lucky enough to be able to afford a cleaner once a week in our household. The truth be told, my parents both worked full-time jobs and having a cleaner wasn't a sign of wealth, it was a choice we had because my parents worked so hard. At any rate, once a week my mum would rudely barge into my room and announce that it was "cleaning day" and request that I at least pick up all of my stuff off the floor, put it into my clothes hamper, away, or stack it on my bed. That way when the cleaner came, she would be able to both see the floor and clean it. Looking back on things it's pretty hard to argue with the logic. I should arguably have been vacuuming my own room but all I had to do was make sure that the floor was clear so that someone else could do it for me. Seemed like a minimal effort but I've already admitted to being a brat. I remember objecting to the idea of "cleaning up" ahead of the "cleaners" arrival. I could have understood the concept if I tried but it wouldn't have helped my argument. I was trying to get out of even the most basic of chores and I would do anything to do it.

My task was realistically a 10 minute job that required limited effort compared to several hours' worth of manual labour each day. What is it that made me such a brat? Am I the only kid that grew up in Australia (or elsewhere in the world) that behaves like this? While in Africa they use an average of 10 Litres of water per day I had access to an unlimited supply and research would suggest that I probably used between 200 and 300 litres per day (the average for someone growing up in the developed world). I didn't need to collect firewood in order to get delicious meals each night. With less disadvantages shouldn't I have been a better rounded person? Surely, with all of those gifts I should have been more willing to help out around the house. I would have been grateful.

Several authors have written extensively on the importance of purpose. I agree wholeheartedly with importance of being clear about your own personal sense of calling or purpose. I think it's critical for every single person. I think that the single greatest source of lasting satisfaction a person can have is a sense that they are "doing the thing that they were put on this planet to do" and you only get that sense of satisfaction if you first and foremost have a sense of what that purpose is in the first place.

Although seeking out your life purpose is a critical task for each of us, I believe that purpose is also important when thinking about the little things in life. For me, the word "purpose" can be explained in one word. Purpose is the answer to the question "Why?" Without purpose a task has no meaning. It's just something we could do. Purpose gives each task a sense of importance and it does it in a way that explains why that task is required. The purpose of collecting that water each day in Africa wasn't so that they can fill up a filtration system in their home. The purpose was to ensure that their household didn't go thirsty each day. Once we install a filtration system, the purpose of that system is to save that household from water-borne diseases. These are fundamentally important things that nobody would question. These purposes are also the kinds of things that someone is likely to believe without question.

At a fundamental level there is purpose in everything we do. Sometimes different people might have different purposes for the one task but there is always an answer to the question "Why?" it's just that some answers are better than others. I would like to think that I was not a fundamentally flawed kid. That I was born just as amazing as each of those kids I've met in Africa. I like to think that being born into their circumstances instead of mine I might have been a lot more dutiful in my chores and less of an ungracious little snot. Of course it's self-serving to suggest this after bringing up that example but I fundamentally believe that we are all born the same. It's ridiculous to suggest that I was born any less amazing than any of those kids. I think the different between their chores and mine was that they had a common sense of purpose that they shared with their family. They all believed that purpose from the bottom of their hearts and as a result very difficult tasks just gets done without fuss. I didn't ever truly understand the purpose of having a house-cleaner as a kid. The reality is that my parents probably invested in this so that they could personally be more available for us kids when they weren't at work. Ask me to sign up to that purpose now and I would do it every day of the week but back then I didn't understand it and I certainly didn't buy into it.

Purpose experienced within our corporate training events

Many people hate team-building activities. I know because historically I was one of those guys. I liked spending time with my team, solving problems together and having some fun but I was always so frustrated by how pointless the tasks seemed. My frustration was typically magnified when the appointed facilitator would try and draw all sorts of conclusions from the activity; many of which I didn't agree with. Sometimes I would walk away from the activity after learning something. However, usually the activity itself was just another trial and tribulation that I had encountered with my team. It was probably worth doing because it brought us together as a team however we were typically galvanised behind a common cynicism of our facilitator and not brought together by anything particularly insightful that they said. I think that when we evaluate something as "pointless" what we are really saying is that I either don't understand or don't agree with the purpose of this activity.

In both the Helping Hands and Water Works Programs we ask people to explore the importance of purpose in each and every activity however it's fairly clear that our activities are not like your average team building experience. For starters both the water filtration systems and hands we make a real things that have a life-changing impact on people. When we ask our participants to focus on quality, we've got a really great reason for doing that! With both programs we start with an activity that is genuinely important.

Once we walk up on that stage, we invest up to 30 minutes in explaining not what the employees are required to do but why that output is really important. We explain that purpose in such a way that everyone understands it in both their head and their heart. We show videos, tell emotional stories, share statistics and answer any questions that people have. Effectively we kick-off the activity with a strong sense of purpose and we take the time to ensure that everyone genuinely believes that purpose in their hearts before proceeding. To emphasise this, I'll sometimes even go as far as to invite people to grab a cup of tea and wander around being a nuisance if they aren't truly excited about getting involved.

During the activity itself there are usually a large range of hurdles that could stump participants. The instructions are better than flat-pack furniture instructions but they are less than ideal. Sometimes groups will have insufficient or duplicate instructions. Often we will wait until people build some momentum before restructuring the teams. Usually we'll apply a disability of some kind to each participant – something that will help them empathise with the people they are trying to help. We never give any training in how to go about the task and although there is only a Helpdesk those staff are instructed to deal with spare-parts related instructions only. Effectively they are not really allowed to help.

What is it that has enabled 7,530 groups of three to build a successful hand despite these challenges? Why have over 600 groups now assembled a water system under difficult circumstances? The reason is simple. It always comes down to purpose.

Whether you are a senior manager, front-line employee or just a parent the single most important thing to communicate in any task is the "purpose". Sure, you need to explain what it is you want that person to deliver to you at the end of the task, but us human beings can cope with an awful lot of ambiguity, change and set-back if we both understand the purpose of the task and believe it in our hearts. Don't believe me? How else could you get a 12 year old kid to find a way to carry a 30 litre container of water 6 kilometres each day?

Purpose-centred task assignment

If you're looking at applying this principle into your own practice as a leader here's a simple task assignment model that you might find helpful. It's based not just on the assumption that purpose is critical. It's also based on the assumption that no task is motivating unless you have a degree of discretion to figure out for yourself how you choose to go about the task. You'll notice that in the below model as a leader you simply do not need to explain "how" to go about the task at all. It's not part of the model. That omission is important as it's backed up be a large volume of research that points towards autonomy and discretion being an important component of motivation in the workplace.

Our simple task assignment model states that there are 5 critical elements to each task:

Situation – Provide the context that is critical for them to understand about this task? Is this just part of a broader project? Is someone else already working on another complementary piece of work? You know that the person you are assigning the task is going to be exercising discretion so try and anticipate some of the information they will need to make good judgements and work productively.

Purpose – Explain why this task is critical. Usually a good purpose statement is no more than 1 sentence long and if you find yourself spending a lot of time on this topic, chances are you're merging some of the "Situation" in with the "Purpose".

Output – Detail very specifically what success will look like. Remember to consider both the quantitative outputs but also any qualitative requirements that you are likely to use when evaluating their work.

Resources – Outline any other forms, tools, employees, research or other materials that the person might find useful.

Time – Always finish by explaining unequivocally when the task needs to be completed by. If the task is a complex project that will result in several outputs then it would usually be a good idea to provide several milestone timeframes in addition to the overall

Although not a formal part of the model, a critical aspect of this working is that *a task is not assigned until it has been understood*. You might carefully craft the most brilliant task in the world and go through that task in thorough detail, not missing a single detail. However, if the person you are communicating with didn't understand all aspects of that task S, P, O, R and T, then you are unlikely to get the outcome that you require.

The idea with the SPORT task assignment model is to start off by preparing your task assignments in writing. Typically this model also works best when you share it with your coworkers. That way, when you miss out on a critical part of the task assignment they will be more likely to point it out and save you both sometime later down the track. A good guide as to whether or not you are ready to begin task assigning verbally is how long and clear your "Purpose" statements are. If you are finding it increasingly easy to get to the nub of "why" a particular task is important and you are finding that those purposes are increasingly successful in motivating your people then it's a good indication that you are ready to try verbal task assignments.

Chapter 6 – Key Insights

- People can overcome many challenges provided they understand "why" the work they are doing is important.
- Understanding the "purpose" of your work is not just an intellectual pursuit, you need to believe it in your heart.
- Good leaders systematically provide a sense of purpose to their people for every task that they assign.
- Use the SPORT task assignment model to practice this in your own workplace.

Chapter 7: Sense of community and belonging

It was New Year's Day, 2014 and Antonia and I had to get up nice and early to get on a flight to Bangalore, India. We had spent the last night of 2013 enjoying the fireworks over Sydney Harbour and at that stage were still planning our wedding which would happen later that year. It was a very happy time and we were both really excited to board our flight. As is always the case when I travel to a far-off land to distribute prosthetic hands I had some interesting luggage. 100 brand new prosthetic hands were packed in my luggage and it was with some relief that Qantas check-in staff were so generous in letting us take so much luggage with us free of charge.

Sure enough as I touched down in Bangalore and took my bags to be x-rayed, 100 pencil cases all packed up and sealed with zip lock bags did draw attention. I always do my best to remain calm under these circumstances as it would be counterproductive to panic. Having said that, each time this happens as a nervous traveler my stomach is doing summersaults. We presented the heavily armed customs official with some documentation and explained what we were doing. The process was escalated (or referred we were not 100% sure) to three separate people before one of the gentlemen we were dealing with informed us that we were free to go. Start to finish it only took about 15 minutes but it felt a lot longer than that in the moment. Interestingly, as I was hastily zipping up my bags again and looking to leave before they changed their mind the very first customs officer that we spoke to began to help me. I was grateful for the assistance but was still under the impression that he didn't understand what the hands were (why else would he have referred my case onto multiple other colleagues). As we finished zipping up the bag and went to go our separate ways the official stopped me and said "Thank you sir for everything you are doing for the people of our country. We are very grateful."

Now I'm a fairly patriotic guy. I definitely think we've got some of the best customs officials in the world, they don't scare you (unless you deserve it) and the process is all very "Australian". However I was struck immediately by the graciousness of this man's comment in India and I think although the process was somewhat stressful, it was my first insight into the sense of community that exists within this highly populated country.

We touched down quite late at night and were actually staying at the Karnataka cricket ground. This was a great honour. The Karnataka state cricket team is traditionally one of the strongest teams in India and is the home of some incredibly gifted world-class players such as Rahul Dravid and Anil Kumble. We didn't arrive at the cricket ground until 2am in the morning and were suspicious that nobody would be available to check us in but sure enough there was a man waiting at the front desk. In fact, there were people everywhere - it's just that they were asleep. Instantly things were put into perspective for us. Not only were our hosts extremely gracious and welcoming but they actually lived and slept at the ground. There were no mattresses that I saw, just some rolled up clothes being used as a pillow while their owners slept on the cold granite floors of the cricket ground. When we checked in and found no toilet-paper we felt embarrassed to once again wake someone up to ask for a spare roll but the gentlemen was happy to help and rushed off to the storeroom. I followed so as to help if I was needed and once again when he opened the door the storeroom there was a young man asleep on the floor in the store-room who jumped to attention and sourced the required supplies. The world is a textured and diverse place. They don't call it "Incredible India" in the tourist commercials for nothing. It's incredible from the second that you touch down and at no stage did I feel anything but welcomed.

There are a number of individual stories from people who received hands on that trip, but one group's story stands out above all in exemplifying the sense of community that I experienced in India. On day three of our fitting trip we were introduced to two little 9 year old boys who had both travelled for half a day to get to the camp that we were working at. Both boys were missing their right hand. We had brought along a few silly little gifts of clip-on koalas to give to kids and so gave them one each. We then asked if they had any friends who might also like one of our gifts and they took us over to a group of 60 children obediently sitting cross-legged on the ground. Looking around the group they could have been straight from one of the most privileged suburbs in any capital city around the world. They were each wearing bright red tailored shorts and short-sleeved white button up shirts. The shorts were bright and clean and the shirts looked like they had been freshly starched and pressed at the dry-cleaners. These kids looked a million bucks (as the saying goes) yet they had all travelled for half a day to get to our camp. I was impressed and busy admiring how adorable they all were as we gave out our gifts but then noticed something else… not a single other boy appeared to have a disability.

In the developed world our kids are no strangers to school excursions. I fondly remember visiting the snowfields and Powerhouse Museum when I was about their age. They were also on a school excursion that day but the entire purpose of that excursion was to accompany their two school-mates to go and get a new hand. These were some of the poorest kids in the world taking incredibly pride in their appearance and travelling for an entire day just to support their classmates get the medical assistance that they needed. My excursions at their age involved being told off in the back of a bus while we went out for some glorified recreation.

The fact is that I could share a similar story about each and every developing country that I've visited. The sense of community in these places is fundamentally different to what I've grown up with. It is true that I will always love the neighbourhood where I was raised and the friends that I made from that area. However would I ever have expected my entire class to come out to the hospital with me if I was ill? I think in the Western world if we are completely honest we experience a form of "picket-fence community". We are willing to accept each other into the family but there are plenty of conditions and if it all goes wrong I can always run back behind my fence. In the developing world, from what I've experienced, you often experience a level of boundariless community. People's lives are so intertwined and independent that it is hard to distinguish between family and friends. In fact the distinction is probably irrelevant for many of those folks.

Boundariless community in the workplace

A strong sense of community is critical when creating an inspired culture. Imagine for a moment that you work in the kind of workplace where you have no need for defenses. Where you feel safe, unconditionally loved and inspired to get involved; not through fear but because you believe so strongly in what your organisation is trying to achieve. Does that sound like the kind of workplace that you would like to operate within?

I think the notion of a boundariless community within the workplace is scary at first and of course to some extent there are always going to be some limits of disclosure and relationship. Having said that, could we all operate more effectively with each other if we knew a bit more about what was going on in each-other's lives? So often when we offend each other in the workplace it's because we've just accidentally touched on a sore point without realizing it. The kind of slip-up that we wouldn't make with family or friends because we know what's going on in their lives. Of course in many respects we can't be friends with everyone, we can't know everything... but would the concept of a boundariless community in your workplace be a step closer to an inspired workplace? I think it would.

When I discuss this notion with clients the first response is normally an inappropriate joke or two about harassment in the workplace. Of course when I talk about the notion of a boundariless community, I'm not talking about a lawless situation. Of course, people should be free to go about their lives in an environment free from harassment, victimisation, discrimination and bullying. That is always the case irrespective of whether you are at work or home. By talking about boundariless community, I'm emphasizing the good. I'm asking you to reach out beyond the task-related interactions we all have to the human being siting behind them. Find out how many kids that person in accounts has. Remember their names. Rather than be afraid of your manager, ask about their life, put yourself in their perspective and empathise with them.

Usually, the only genuine reticence behind embracing a boundariless community in the workplace is the fear that somehow we will lose the ability to reward and recognise people differentially. That somehow the notional of unconditional love in the workplace is inconsistent with judging people on merit for promotional opportunities and such. I see these two concepts as completely independent however I completely understand why people share the same fear. I think that in the modern workplace we have become way too obsessed with "leadership and management training" and forgotten the importance of building truly trusting relationships with our co-workers and employees. We've forgotten that leadership is essentially a relational construct. You're only a leader if you can influence others to gladly follow you and typically you're only able to do that in the long-term if you've build a trusting and genuine relationship with each of your team.

Feedback in a boundariless environment

Most of us have been through "how to give feedback" training courses. Of course there are various methods that are taught as part of front-line management courses but my favourite is affectionately known as the "shit sandwich". Most of us would be familiar with what this is. The concept is that a clever manager will always open with a compliment before letting the employee know what they really think of them, before then finishing the conversation with another complement or something positive. This process is simple and efficient but it's not effective and it makes the leader comes across as inauthentic. Giving and receiving feedback is just one of many concepts that we have allowed ourselves to believe is simply a training issue.

The fact is, if you have a true relationship with your manager where you feel like they "get you" and you feel like you can trust them, all of a sudden receiving feedback takes on an entirely new perspective. When a friend brings something up because they care of course we might feel defensive, but we know that there's no need to be afraid of the feedback that's coming our way. Our survival instincts don't kick in and we are so much more likely to be able to hear what is being said. Of course in a true relationship we are not just going to hear from the boss when we've done something wrong, we're going to hear from him or her frequently. We're going to be in each other's lives. We are going to know about important dates and other stressors that might be going on in our lives. BEFORE that manager walks into our office to give us that feedback, they have already made a number of deposits into our emotional bank account and we don't feel affronted that they are coming to us today. On top of all of that this manager gets you, the way they go about the conversation with you is entirely tailored to you as a person so they don't accidentally push on your hot buttons. They don't pick the wrong location or timing. Everything just goes more smoothly as a result if that fantastic relationship you have with your manager.

"What planet are YOU on?" I hear you ask... Most of us have only experienced one or two managerial relationships like that in our lives. They are sadly uncommon. However, for those of us that have had one of those relationships with their manager you can remember just how loyal you were to them. You know how much longer you stayed in that role as a result and you know what lengths you would have gone to for that person. Having a true sense of community in the workplace is critical to creating the kind of environment where we can all thrive. It's a critical part of the journey towards an inspired workplace.

We have all tried to delicately peel off a Band-Aid (or first aid bandage) off our skin after it's been stuck there for a day or so. It's painful stuff... especially if it's been placed somewhere with a couple of hairs. As kids we learn that the best way to do this is to tear it off quickly, the pain is significant, but it's short-lived as opposed to the elongated torture of slowly peeling off that bandage. As leaders, we frequently come across situations that require us to act quickly. If revenues have fallen dramatically, it is sometimes better to cut costs quickly than to slowly reduce staffing numbers over time. At least if you "take the pain" early it gives people more time to recover whereas a slower approach might leave people anxious and "survivor syndrome" starts kicking in. It is definitely true to say that sometimes, as a leader in the workplace, the quickest approach is the best even if it's a bit more painful in the short-term.

Building effective community in the workplace is not one of those things that can be achieved quickly. In fact, one of the recurrent themes within this book is that sometimes the best and most sustainable way to go about things is actually the most difficult. It takes time to build genuine relationships with people at work. It takes an emotional investment and each time you try and foster a new relationship you're making yourself emotionally vulnerable. It's much easier to give someone a "shit sandwich" feedback session, take a deep breath, then go back to your desk and congratulate yourself that you "ripped it off like a Band-Aid". The problem is your feedback was probably not really heard. All the person really heard in your interaction was that you were inauthentic and didn't say what you really meant. You just made a withdrawal from the emotional bank account of that employee and it might take some time to build up your balance with them again.

Chapter 7 – Key Insights

- Having a strong sense of community is critical to shaping an inspired culture
- We should strive to create an environment where our people feel safe and unconditionally loved.
- Boundariless relationships in the workplace are a good thing.
- Leaders can still give feedback about opportunities for improvement within an inspired culture.
- However, leadership is a relational construct and you have to "earn the right" to give someone feedback without them getting defensive.

Chapter 8: The limits of competitiveness

As previously mentioned, many local villagers in the developing world depend on the barter system. When you're living in relative poverty, the local currency just has far less value to you than a bag of rice, loaf of bread or piece of fruit. As a result, local villagers will often swap goods and services rather than using the local currency. Of course the barter system reveals a fundamentally different way of determining value. However, I think it also reveals a fundamentally different social approach we could all learn from.

When a local villager decides to swap two bags of avocados for one bag of onions, they are of course negotiating a business deal of sorts. However the act of barter isn't just a pure business transaction, it's a transaction that will typical strengthen the relationship between two neighbours. Perhaps the value of avocados will fluctuate throughout the year but in a true two-way relationship those neighbours will not always be motivated purely from a supply and demand perspective. They are neighbours. They live life together and want each other to succeed. Their kids go to school together. They depend on the same water sources, the same roads and the same medical centres. Relationships in the developing world are based on these kind of raw essentials of life. Of course, politics creeps into every culture. Jealousy, dishonesty and vanity are a part of every culture. However, at the end of the day, community members need to help each other out to survive. They are fundamentally more collaborative because they have to be. However, it's also a cultural norm passed down over the generations. The very concept of where one family starts and another begins is far more vague because the value of individuality and competition is simply not emphasised as much in such cultures.

Of course, many of the villages I've visited also have a marketplace where currency is valued over goods and services. Most local farmers will also sell goods at such markets and stalls in addition to bartering with their neighbours. At the marketplace, competition is obviously the order of the day. If you have a good or service that is scarce you will demand top dollar for such a resource. As a result, your purchasing power is significantly greater than your neighbours'. You win and they lose. Later in the year those fortunes might be

A local marketplace in Uganda

reversed. In the developing world, inequitable access to resources isn't just a blow to someone's ego, it can be a life or death matter and tears at the very fabric of a community. Although there will always be a place for the market in remote villages, it is also true to say that it is necessary but insufficient to sustain a community. If you took the individualistic cultures of Australia or the USA and imported it, without adjustment, into such a community the results would be catastrophic. Truly, a collaborative culture is not just a quaint characteristic of such villages, it's a necessity.

Too cool to keep to ourselves - we want to share it with the world!

During my very first meeting with the global founder of the Helping Hands Program he shared with me that "this initiative is just too cool to keep to ourselves and we want to give it to the world." It was a statement that instantly resonated with me. If I was going to get involved in charity work why would I want to keep that all to myself? Why wouldn't I share it with as many people as possible? To do anything else than that would surely result in fewer hands being made and ultimately less people getting the help that they need. It was only natural that when I ultimately accepted an invitation to become the Australasian distributor for the Helping Hands Program my mind was immediately on how we could invite as many people as possible to get involved in the program.

In my experience, most people who become involved in team-building and experiential learning often have an outdoor education background or are specialist learning and development professionals. They are typically fantastic facilitators and are looking to capitalize on that strength within the team-building market. That wasn't my motivation at all. Although I had been a formally trained facilitator during a previous role and had facilitated a large range of leadership and business meetings I didn't see this as my core strength. I honestly just felt that the Helping Hands Program would be a great way to get involved in a worthwhile cause. I also knew that it was the single most powerful leadership and learning tool I had come across in over 10 years of working in the field. Perhaps that is another reason why I naturally looked to grow the program via partnership with others. From the very first day that we launched the program my mantra was "We can never find ourselves saying no to or building barriers that prevent anyone who wants to build a hand. The second we start to do that with this program we will have lost our way."

The idea of inviting as many people as possible to build a hand seems obvious at first glance. However, it's not the prevailing norm within the corporate team-building market. Within the first month of launching I began to reach out to all of those other companies who were involved in philanthropic teambuilding in one way or another at the time. I wanted to propose the concept of starting an informal "community of practice" where we might get together on a regular basis, share ideas, help each other out and of course refer customers to each other when we had a past client looking for a new idea. Once again, this seemed like such an obvious thing to do. If there were a number of companies just like me who were motivated to make a difference then I had no problem whatsoever in sharing the news about their projects. Of course when you've built a hand one year and had a great experience it stands to reason that next year you might be looking for a different experience and I wanted to have a good network of contacts to refer those customers to.

To say that I was underwhelmed by the response is an understatement in itself. There was no response. Not a single person returned my calls or emails. People saw me as a competitor and were so defensive that not a single contact chose to even respond. You see the prevailing mindset as I can see it in the corporate team-building market is to defend your Intellectual Property closely and to compete aggressively with alternative opportunities.

So although it seems obvious that if you're going to get involved in a charity program you're going to do everything in your power to maximise your contribution to that charity, it seems like most organisations out there also think it's obvious that the best way to maximise their contribution is to compete with others. I think that many of us, especially those raised in quite individualistic cultures like Australia, America or the UK are raised to believe that the only way to win is by beating someone else. There can be no winners without losers. We're raised to believe that life is just like a sports-game and the second we clarify our goals we immediately begin to look around and see who we need to beat in order to achieve that goal.

Competition within our workshops

Anyone that has ever participated in a Helping Hands workshop would know that before I even begin I announce that "there are no winners or losers today except for the real customers that will benefit from our work. We are not in competition today and I want you to help each other out as much as possible to do a good job for those customers." I then always set the primary goal for the day at the overall group level. Essentially the goal is always to "build all of the hands in the room" or to have "10 happy customers at the end of this exercise". I never assign the task as "each group is to build the hand that has been allocated to them". Of course the subtext of what I'm saying to each individual is that would be a failure if all you do is build the hand that is in front of you in the allotted times while other teams struggle. Often I'll even go as far during my activity briefing to make that explicit by pointing out that "if we don't provide all of the customers that we've set out to help with a hand then that would definitely constitute a failure for every single person in this room."

The results of this briefing are surprising to most people but extremely predictable to me and other experienced facilitators. Despite my briefing, during the first 30 minutes of almost every activity, participants will tunnel-vision on the hand immediately in front of them and will usually limit their interactions to only their immediate team members. Of course by doing this they are making a number of big assumptions. That is, that someone has divided up the hands equally, that all of the hands

96

have already been distributed and by working individually on the hand in front of them, they have stumbled across the most efficient and effective way to get this job done (despite the fact that they haven't brainstormed other ways of approaching the task). Depending on my client's budget and the way we have tailored the activity for that particular client, those assumptions will sometimes be entirely incorrect. The client might have purchased an extra 10% of hands as a stretch target. Some employee's might have called in sick leaving unequal group sizes. Sometimes I'll have a big pile of hands sitting on the stage and will wave them around as an example of what each person's kit looks like then ask people to build all of the hands in the room. People's first reaction is almost always to turn immediately to the hand in front of them and focus on a different task to the one I assigned them. As soon as that happens I know that it is unlikely that the group will ever come back to that pile of hands at the front of the room. It's an incredibly predictable phenomena. Today, after 700 workshops, perhaps 2 groups have challenged these assumptions at the beginning of the task and had a meaningful conversation to check how the group wanted to approach the task. It was no surprise that one of those same groups was also the quickest group ever to finish all hands in the room.

Of course you might say that we have set up these teams for failure by not explicitly pointing out all of the potential pitfalls before they begin the activity. You might argue that we should have appointed leaders within the room and then we would have had more chance of better planning to emerge. Both of these observations would be correct. However, there's also something else going on in the room. Once again, after over 700 workshops there is another phenomena that occurs during about 90% of those workshops. That is the phenomena of the "winning team". Irrespective of the fact that I've announced several times during the activity that it's a group-wide task, that the only winners and losers are our customers, that team that finishes first will almost always rush up to me as a facilitator and let me know that they have completed. Other groups will go as far as to strap the hand on themselves and write "We Won" on a piece of paper and wave it around in front of their colleagues. In each of these cases the "Winning Team" has missed the point. Of course it is an important milestone to acknowledge when the first group has finished but it's not an important milestone because someone has "won". It's important because at that point in time we know that there is a lot of knowledge in the room. We know at that point that there are at least 3 people in the overall group that know how to solve every aspect of the task. So this is an important potential tipping point for the group because from that time onwards the larger group can be entirely self-sufficient. They know that there is not a single problem that they need external advice about. Of course the opportunity for the "winning team" to be effective technical experts within their overall group is often wasted if they choose to spend all of their energy gloating in front of their colleagues.

I actually think it's the good in people, not the bad, that makes us tunnel vision a little bit on the task immediately in front of us. When you think about it, those people who sprint towards the finishing line and try and make that hand as quickly as possible are not doing a bad job. Chances are they are motivated out of the goodness of their heart. Chances are they care deeply about the work that they are doing. They are likely extremely engaged in the activity. However, a funny thing happens when you're highly engaged in your work. When we are highly engaged that's actually when we are most at risk of our blinkers coming on and focusing a bit too much on just the task that's immediately before us. We might know that we can ask for help from other teams but we also want to solve the problem ourselves, to get to the end of the task and feel that sense of pride that from experience comes when you solve the problem by yourself. We want to go home and tell the people we love about what we've achieved and share that feeling with them. There's nothing terrible about being that motivated about your work. There's nothing wrong with feeling pride in what you've achieved. Except that in my experience it does get in the way of effective collaboration. Not always, but sometimes when the blinkers come on, it blinds us to opportunities that we otherwise might see. Truly, it's the good in people, not the bad that generally makes us compete. The challenge is that when we are super engaged in our work we are also most at risk of tunnel-visioning and potentially working in silos.

Designing for collaboration

I think it's fair to say that within our culture there is an underpinning assumption that a competitive approach is always the best way to go about the task at hand and in my experience that is simply not true. When we established both the Helping Hands and Water Works Program we actually built both projects on the basis of an assumption that collaborating would be the best way to proceed. That assumption has proven to be correct. Now, five years later, over half of the hands and water systems that we donate are actually made by other facilitators or team-building companies. That enables us to run an increasingly large project in an incredibly cost-effective way. As I write this book, we only employ one full-time logistics coordinator yet are making up to 600 hands and 200 water filtration systems per month. Our scalability and potential growth into the future is not limited by our own capacity. We now have an ever growing army of facilitators out there building hands and water filtration systems and I honestly believe there's potential for us to solve both of these huge global problems one day. Now those staunch proponents of "competition in the workplace" will argue that I couldn't possibly know for sure that I've had more success by going down the path I have -except I do know that. Helping Hands is a global initiative where specific organisations take the lead for various regions around the globe. I know that my region is the only place in the world where we have rolled out the initiative in this manner. I also know that my region builds 4 times as many hands per capita as any other country in the world.

Almost every organisation that I've worked in talks about the need to "break down internal silos" and adopt a truly collaborative approach. However, just like any significant cultural change project, such a goal is easier said than done. To truly achieve a collaborative culture you have to do more than hold a great training event (although that's a good start), you also need to realign your leadership behaviour, organisational processes, and measurement systems to all reinforce a culture of collaboration. That kind of work might sound "warm and fuzzy" but it's actually truly hard work that will permeate every aspect of your organisation. Allow me to elaborate by once again using the Helping Hands and Water Works Projects as an example.

When launching both projects we could have done so as a philanthropic arm my consulting business. We did in fact consider that approach for some time. In fact, to keep costs down for the first year or two Helping Hands was offered as a service by my consulting business. There were some upsides to such an approach. I did have a successful business with plenty of potential clients to sell the idea to. However, we also knew that involving the name of our consulting business might discourage other consulting businesses and facilitators from getting involved. It wasn't the best way to say to the market that we wanted to truly collaborate so instead, as soon as we could afford to do so, we incorporated a new independent entity to run both programs. That single decision would have wide-reaching implications. However, there are also a range of other decisions we had to make to complement that decision:

- Although we have registered both of the trademarks Water Works Program ™ and Helping Hands Program ™ and have a wealth of intellectual property developed for both projects, we allow facilitators complete access to all of our IP. We call it our "open-source approach to IP". Of course we reserve the right to refuse any partner from using our trademarks in ways that we believe will harm the project but to this date we have not had to invoke this veto right.

- When participants receive giveaways, assembly manuals or anything else during the program all reference materials and collateral refers back to our project websites and those project websites are always written in a way that reinforces the legitimacy of all facilitators.

- We never say no to a self-facilitator that wants to get involved. Even if they see themselves as our direct competitor. If getting them involved will result in a single hand being built that wouldn't otherwise be built, then we welcome them with open arms.

- Our tracking website (3billionstories.com) was commissioned in April in order to provide absolute transparency regarding where each of the donations made as part of our program goes. When we designed this website, we designed it to be "brand agnostic". What we mean by this is that we have actively avoided hardwiring links back to either the Water Works Program or Helping Hands. That is because we want our self-facilitators to get the repeat business and goodwill that naturally comes from getting involved in our projects. We want to help grow their business, not ours.

Of course all of those design elements have been critical to reinforcing a collaborative approach with other organisations. These are not "fuzzy" or ambiguous decisions that we have made. They each involved deep reflection and clarity of vision, but when it came down to implementing them, it involved a lot of hard detail-focused work.

There are a lot of problems in the world that are best dealt with by taking a competitive approach. Often self-interest in a deeply competitive environment can result in incredible innovation and productivity. I'm certainly not arguing with this valid perspective. I'm just positing that not every problem is best solved with a bias towards competition.

Does an organisation that you care about extoll the virtues of collaboration but fall a tiny bit short? We are all involved in organisations that depend on collaboration. Perhaps it's your workplace or a community group. Either way I can guarantee that the majority of people involved are probably working with the best of intentions to work together and help each other out as best they can. The reality is that within the developed world a competitive perspective is so deeply ingrained for many of us that we find ourselves competing without even realising it. Perhaps our ego is bruised and we find ourselves trying to win an argument. Perhaps it's less obvious and we've simply designed a task in such a way that has pitted one group against another without even realising.

Being cooperative just doesn't come naturally to many of us and admitting that is the first step towards truly leveraging the collective capability of many organisations.

Chapter 8 - Key Insights

- Competition can be useful in many different contexts but it is not always the best way of going about things.
- Many of us like to compete as a default mode of operating and it is often difficult for us to identify where a more cooperative approach would be better.
- If you are seeking to create a more collaborative culture in your workplace then you need to do more than write a good compelling speech. You must utilise all of the tools at your disposal that were discussed in Chapter 4.
- Critically, a cooperative culture isn't just a "warm and fuzzy" idea it's something that good leaders shape with carefully considered cultural intervention.

Chapter 9: The primacy of family and importance of work-life integration

I've previously spoken about the notion of family in the developing world. In Uganda multiple generations will usually share the one house. That house usually only consists of one or two rooms and those "rooms" might just be separated with a curtain. The house itself is usually made of mud and/or mud-bricks. Either way, it will have been constructed by the family itself and people have a real attachment to it. Of course in the developed world we would also refer to our grandparents and cousins as "family" but would we live under the same roof? Close friends and neighbours might also be referred to as "family" and invited to stay. Even if those friends do not sleep at the family home they might spend a lot of time there during the day and often they might be referred to as "family" if you ask.

Not only is the concept of family much more inclusive and variable, people identify with their families in a very different way. As the children grow up and find marital partners of their own they will often choose to live with their parents. As those newlyweds have children, the names of the parents are usually changed from that point onwards to reflect the name of the first-born child. For example my mother's name is Jane but as soon as I was born her name would have been changed to Mumma Matthew. So the concept of family is not just valued within the family-unit but it becomes the way that parents are defined in their communities.

It is because of this relatively inclusive and permeable definition of family that we from the developed world often have difficulty finding a common language to talk about issues of family and community. The two are inextricably linked and not distinguished in the same way that we would in the west. When we register each water system that is donated we always ask how many people "live in the household" because we find that this is a much more stable concept that is easier to define.

People in the developing world don't just define family in a different way to us, they will also resort to desperate measures to protect that family. I've been privileged to have an opportunity to fit hands to 87 people India so far. The local fitting teams have fitted literally thousands more than I and what they all tell me is that the number one reason for people losing their hand is due to electrocution. During my trip 26% of hand recipients had lost hands this way and I'm told that this is a representative sample of what goes throughout the rest of the country and in many other parts of the developing world.

When I think about electrical accidents in the developed world I'm immediately reminded that most of us have these ingenious little devices fitted to our switchboards called "safety switches". Effectively, the power grid in your home detects when someone might have been shocked and immediately cuts off the power before too much damage can be done. I experienced this situation one day whilst using my electrical hedger in the front-yard. I was sweating and tired and before I knew it had cut through the very power-cord that I was holding. I didn't even feel a shock. Power was immediately cut off and my stupidity didn't lead towards permanent injuries. Other common electrical accidents in Australia include people forgetting to check with their utilities company before excavating a large hole in their backyard, potentially installing home insulation over the top of wiring in a dangerous way or screwing a new hook into the wall without first cutting off electricity to the area.

These are not the kind of accidents that people have in the developing world. As I understand it, the single biggest cause of electrocution amongst our hand recipients are people that are so desperate to power their homes that they resort to trying to steal electricity from the grid. How might you go about such a thing? My understanding is that you need to first either dig up or pull down a cable. Of course even this process can be fraught if there is even the smallest blemish to the insulation of the cable. If you are digging perhaps equipment penetrates the cable. Once you've revealed the cable, you then hold your extension cable over the top of that electrical main, grab a steel bolt (similar to what we use in our Helping Hands Programs) then hit that steel bolt with a hammer attempting to close the circuit in one blow by going through both the extension cable and electrical main. Of course if you release the bolt at exactly the right time and manage to ensure that there is no recoil of the cabling as a result of the blow then you've just managed to secure power for your home.

Of course this whole process is extremely dangerous. It's entirely possible for such incidents to be fatal and losing a hand is one of the best outcomes when the procedure fails. People all over the developing world take huge risks every day. During one week in India I met two different young boys who had lost their hands playing with dynamite. Why? Their parents work in a quarry and bringing your own dynamite to and from work is one of those expectations. I guess we could liken it to the expectation that a plumber will bring his own tools to your house when he comes to fix your pipes. It's just that these people have to go to a quarry and their main tools are explosives. Kids are the same all around the world. I am certain that as a 13 year old boy, if my parents were storying dynamite at our house, I would have tried to play with it at some point. Maybe I would have shown some restraint for a year or so but eventually the lure of being able to blow something up would have been too much. Those two kids I met were no different to me. It's just that their parents needed to keep dynamite at home in order to keep their jobs. Given the same temptation I would have done exactly the same thing that they did.

When I first tell each of these stories people often express a degree of annoyance at the people concerned. How stupid for someone that is not a licensed electrician to try and steal power from the grid! Bringing dynamite home was like tempting fate and a sensible parent would never do such a thing. Is this really the case?

Kids are the same all around the world. So are parents. When my wife and I start our own family I'm pretty sure that I will be willing to take the odd risk if I feel it will benefit my family. Those parents bringing dynamite into their home were only doing so because it was a requirement of their jobs. Of course that job was also probably the only reason why the family lived in relative comfort with a food and shelter. Of course they could decide to get another job but would you be willing to take such a risk when you know that jobs are few and far between? If we think about the lighting example, how many evening meals have you shared around the table with your family after the sun has gone down? Do you kids ever have to study after hours? Do you and your family feel like that you get a lot out of reading at night before bed? With light comes education, valuable family time and safety. Having light is something we truly take for granted in the developed world. It's always just been there but if you lost it one day and there was no other option but to take a risk for your family how desperate would you be?

There are other ways for people to light their homes. Often this involves using paraffin lamps or candles. Of course the people who are using such lamps are not usually living in fire-proof homes so this is dangerous in itself. However, I think that the most obvious tragedy in the developing world that I've witnessed is the number of kids who have clearly experienced significant burns as the result of accidents with candles and lamps. It's truly tragic stuff.

Differing concepts of family

I would not be brave enough to argue that family is more important in the developing world than it is here. I'd be afraid of what my own mother would say (just joking mum). However, as I reflect on how often we in the west celebrate and demonstrate the importance of family it is a little confronting. If you are like me, your family is everything to you and there is nothing you enjoy more than spending time with extended family and living life together. Having said that, in contrast, I was often encouraged to put my career first when I was growing up. It was never a problem if I couldn't answer a call because I was in a meeting or similar. These are just little things but I know that as I've grown up at various times in my career I've definitely put myself first.

In many ways, we have built-in structures in our society that protect and defend the importance of family. Mothers and Father's days, public holidays, carer's leave and bereavement leave are all examples in the developed world where we've chosen to put family first. However, I wonder if being more truly personal and integrative might be what's called for.

You see in the modern world concepts of work-life balance are already giving way to work-life integration. Gone are the days where you would finish your work for the day when you left the office. My wife is a media advisor and every morning she gets up at 5:30am to review the news of the day before going back to bed. She then arises an hour or so later to go to work and if she receives any media inquiries she begins work from home. Many people nowadays have very similar jobs. The rise of smart-phones has made such a trend almost irreversible but is this is a good thing and what should we be doing about it?

I believe that family should always come first. If you are lucky enough to grow up with a family as fantastic as mine is then that's something worth defending. However, the time for defending that via clearly defined forms of leave and public holidays is gone in my view. If you expect your employee to answer a work call once they get home, then you should equally expect them to answer a personal call while at work. In the same way that our friends in the developing world don't draw such a firm definition of who is and is not a member of their family, we should not be seeking to draw clear, black and white, distinctions between work and life. There are some roles where people are rostered for every minute of every day. There are also other roles where the distraction a telephone call here and there would be a genuine health and safety risk. However, for all of us that don't fall under either of these categories I think a more permeable approach to work-life balance is required; we need to look towards work-life integration.

Work-life integration for me isn't a set of employment policies. It's a much more deeply personal concept. I believe that we should aspire to work for employers who share our hopes and dreams. I believe that everyone deserves to feel as great about what they do as I get to. Sure there are a lot of jobs that we need done in the world and they vary dramatically. We can't all get involved in charity work to the extent that I do, else we'd run out of money to fund that kind of thing. Thankfully everyone on the planet is unique. I believe that there is enough diversity in the world (both amongst the people looking for work and those with great jobs to fill) that we can make this happen.

Once you find that job that isn't just acceptable but makes your soul sing or you find a job where you truly believe you're involved in fulfilling your life's purpose then that's half of the challenge. I also think that we need to completely redesign our workplaces to promote work-life integration and it starts with the very DNA of modern-day workplaces – job descriptions. Ever since the industrial revolution we've tried to divide and conquer various jobs into the narrowest and most clearly defined tasks that we can then assign to people. It's why we create job descriptions - to define what people should and should not be doing. Can't define a job narrowly? That's ok, we just have to call that person a manager and pay them a tiny bit more. Taking a step beyond job descriptions, process maps are a similar attempt to define how various roles are supposed to interact with people. The problem with all of this industrial revolution thinking is that if you can define every job and every process that well in today's age then ultimately the best way to get it done isn't with a human being, chances are there's an app, robot or computer for that!

Work-life integration in the workplaces of the future

There are several guiding principles that are going to be important when leading the workplaces of the future:

(1) *Know your people.* ATTEMPTING to understand your employees' hopes and dreams is simply not good enough today. You need to need to understand each individual's values,

112

beliefs and dreams to such an extent that you know how they will respond in various situations.

(2) *Err on the side of generosity* when it comes to personal leave, flexibility for family requirements and safety-related concerns. It might feel tough at first but you will reap the rewards of this strategy many times over if you are truly generous to your people regarding the matters that they really care about.

(3) *Don't get fixated on defining where the workplace starts and finishes.* Empower people to capitalise on inspiration wherever and whenever it takes hold. Who cares if someone walked through the night and didn't turn up the next day?! If just one idea that they had overnight has the potential to change the whole direction of your company then who are you to get fixated on the fact that they weren't at their desk at 9am?

(4) *Be very clear on the OUTPUT that you want each employee to deliver.* Of course everyone needs a bit of guidance and support about how to go about their job at first but make sure that your guidance is not limiting their thinking as well. You want your people thinking creatively wherever possible and if a new idea comes to them while they are shuffling peas around a plate at home that night... even better!

(5) *Be very clear about WHY each assignment is important.* Explaining what output you are expecting is an important piece of the puzzle but it's not the part which typically inspires your team. Try investing in explaining why a task is so important to see your team's motivation truly come to life.

Of course work-life integration is not directly correlated with employee engagement and ultimately effort but it's closely related. I believe that the success of your work-life integration efforts will be most closely related to the employee's emotional well-being. That is, the extent to which they feel happy, demonstrate healthy thinking patterns and are resilient against unanticipated challenges.

The relationship between employee well-being, engagement at work and the way that this impacts on an employee's effort in the workplace is relatively complex. An individual's level of engagement is shaped by a clear sense of purpose, empowerment and the extent to which they feel that they are growing. In other words, each of those three key drivers is independent of an employee's general level of well-being. However, if an employee is anxious or depressed, because of some personal matters outside of work, this is almost definitely going to impact on the level of discretionary effort that they exercise at work.

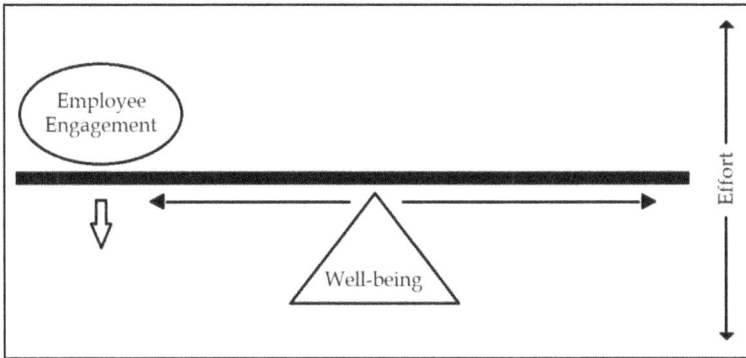

I believe that the nature of the relationship between well-being and engagement is best described using a see-saw analogy. We all know that the greater an employee's engagement, the greater the level of discretionary effort an employee is likely to exercise. In terms of a see-saw, if a great big dose of engagement sits one end of the see-saw, the other end is likely to go up. We think that employee well-being is like the fulcrum of that see-saw. It won't change the direction of the relationship between engagement and effort however as you move that fulcrum left or right it is certainly going to impact on the amount of leverage a company gets from employee engagement. For those academics reading this book, in a statistical sense, well-being is a "moderating variable" which impacts on the relationship between employee engagement and discretionary effort.

As always, there is no single magic solution that enables leaders to shape an inspired workplace but having a well-developed understanding of family is critical. Not only should leaders be looking to shape an environment where their workplace is a home away from home, we also believe that it's not possible for a leader to truly lead in the workplace without understanding what's going on in life for each of their employees.

Chapter 9 – Key Insights

-   The workplaces of the future will embrace family and work towards an increasingly integrated approach which doesn't pit workplace needs against those of family.
-   Work-life integration requires a workplace where leaders: Know their people; Err on the side of generosity; Don't get fixated on defining the workplace; Are clear about the OUTPUT they require from their team; and Are clear about WHY each assignment is important.
-   Employee engagement and motivation are intrinsically linked to the emotional well-being of your people.

Chapter 10: Innovation

As we were driving to Katoma, Uganda I was a little bit confused by seeing a large number of relatively plain looking monuments. In my experience they looked a little bit like the kinds of graves and tombs that you see in rural Vietnam and it took me a day or two to build up the courage to ask about them. I certainly didn't want to run the risk of offending anyone. They effectively look like an organised pile of brown bricks. Not too dissimilar to ancient ruins in South-East Asia but something about them made me think that they weren't anywhere near as old.

When I finally asked about what these piles of bricks were I was a little disappointed to find that they were actually kilns for making bricks. All of the buildings in Katoma are made out of either mud or mud bricks. There are a few different methods to build a mud hut and one of those involves using mud bricks that have been fired in a kiln for additional longevity and strength. Once again, these kilns are just powered by firewood gathered from the local surrounds and there is nothing elaborate about the construction of the kilns. They are made out of mud-bricks themselves. I have to assume that building a hut with mud-bricks would be simpler or longer lasting than other methods but it's not the most common method as far as I could see. If you ever get a chance, look up "how to build a mud hut" on either YouTube or Google. Either way you will likely find it as fascinating as I did. The quality of mud-hut construction is surprisingly good. This form of construction is water-proof, made from renewable materials and is a great insulator against the heat. It is truly astonishing what people can achieve using just the materials that they have at their disposal.

Of course building their own shelters is just the tip of the ice-berg in terms of the ingenuity folks in the developing world exhibited while I was visiting. Our water filtration systems are effectively two separate buckets, connected by a tube. One bucket needs to be positioned below the other because the whole system is gravity fed. The lower bucket also has a tap in it so that you can easily access the clean, filtered water. Naturally once both buckets are full they are incredibly heavy and difficult to move. The lower the buckets are the more likely it is that they will be contaminated by either the soil or animals roaming nearby. At any rate this is a challenge that still needs to be overcome when we give our filtration system to each family. The reality is that each of those families will be able to use the system from day-one. The optimal set-up for each household will be different depending on the space they have available and lay-out of their home.

We have now been back to Katoma twice. During the first visit we were obviously distributing the systems initially and people hadn't decided yet where they would put their system or precisely how they might set it up. As a result during that first we witnessed a lot of creative, short-term solutions to the problem. One family had put the system on their dining table. This might make sense but it wasn't just their dining table it was their only table. Taking up precious real-estate there might not have been the best long-term solution. Another family had taken a carton that they used to collect recycled glass bottles. In this part of the world they still use glass coke bottles and instead of melting them down and setting them again each use they simply wash them back at the factory before sending them to the shop again. Local people receive a small recompense for saving up and returning the bottles and the system works incredibly well. I was very taken by this particular set-up, partially because it was so similar to what we might see in modern-day design but in a very different way. One of the popular trends in modern kitchen design is to integrate a wine-rack somewhere in the kitchen. Maybe it's instead of some shelves at head-height, maybe it's at the end of a breakfast bar. Either way, a lot of kitchens are being designed in this way and people are paying top dollar for the privilege of having such a decadent statement incorporated into their kitchen lay-out. In a very unique way this man had actually mirrored modern kitchen design in his own way. Once again there was a wine-rack incorporated into his kitchen it just so happened that this rack held empty soft-drink bottles (not vintage wine).

During the second trip to Katoma our team was very excited to report back that each and every system was being used in the way that it was intended and that they had observed a marked decline in water-borne illnesses as a result of those gifts. One of the things I was particularly excited to see was that during the 6 months since the systems had been donated each and every family had built a more permanent stand to hold the water system. Some of these were built with solid wood and nails that looked like it had been sourced from a local timber mill but most of the stands were 100% abbreviated and made from wood collected in the local area, then strapped together with twine and other materials found locally. These structures were successfully holding up to 40 litres of water and were made with the most primitive of resources and tools.

The old adage that "necessity is the mother of invention" could never be truer than in the developed world. Much of the innovation that is done at a grass roots level in Uganda is motivated by a basic need for survival. Our water systems are incredibly valuable to any family that has ever experienced a water-borne disease or worse-still, lost a loved one as a result of such a disease. Our system instantly becomes one of the most valuable things these families possess yet it does require a bit of personal innovation in order to make it work ideally for each family.

As a part of the broader Water Works project we have debated many times whether or not to include the cost of a small stand being made by local carpenters in the area. Such stands would be relatively affordable and would also help give a boost to the local economy. The problem is that they would also increase the cost of a sponsorship and might result in a reduction in the overall number of water systems our program is able to provide to people in need. These kinds of dilemmas are always tricky and regrettably common when working in the charity sector.

One of the points that is normally the casting vote in favour of not sponsoring all of the stands is that the requirement for each individual family to put in some effort and build a stand has a really positive by-product. Effectively the family's sense of ownership increases dramatically. They value the gift even more so than they previously did. Another related aspect of this problem is the need for families to be able to self-maintain the system. When we donate the systems we do a lot more than pass it over and wish the family well. We always hold a seminar where we explain how to use the systems, the importance of hygiene and also some basic maintenance tips for the systems. We even provide the tools required to cut holes in new buckets in the event that their first bucket springs a leak. Effectively the family would be back up and running in a matter of minutes… all they need is a new bucket or two. Being able to maintain and fix things in the developing world is incredibly important. It's not just a more affordable and sustainable way of running a charity project, it's also an important way of building ownership.

At different stages during my travels I've crossed paths with several organisations that provide wheelchairs to disadvantaged people in the developing world. Such charities are doing incredibly important work and although we are not currently involved in any such projects we would love to have an opportunity to do so at some stage in the future. When you talk to such organisations they will often share how the most expensive wheelchair in the developed world can easily be completely useless in a developing world context. Some examples that they have shared with me include the fact that if a chair is made of titanium, carbon or another expensive composite material then it might well be a very light device, but it will be almost impossible for local tradespeople to obtain the materials required to fix anything that goes wrong with it. The best case scenario is that the wheelchair owner will end up with a half titanium: half steel chair and that such a device would be unbalanced, unsafe and difficult to steer. In addition, wheelchair wheels over here will often be a combination of small wheels at the front of the chair and large ones at the back. Such an arrangement is tailor made to an environment where you might be travelling on prepared surfaces and indoor flooring but as soon as you take that arrangement and transport it into an environment where the user is wheeling around on dirt paths and the like it's entirely unsatisfactory. As a result, the design of a wheelchair in Cambodia that I was particularly impressed with was completely different to what we would expect in the developing world. Often they are built with bicycle wheels. These are perfect because it's easy to get a replacement. They are also typically quite wide which helps the chair from not sinking into the dirt or grass. Finally, there are typically only 3 wheels and there is often a separate hand-crank option to propel the chair forwards. That way the individual doesn't need to touch the wheels which tend to get a lot dirtier in the developing world without the luxury of footpaths and roads everywhere you go.

Once again, necessity is the mother of invention and I have no doubt that the unique features our partners in Cambodia have built into their chairs make them more fit for the purpose that they were intended whilst also making them more likely to be accepted and used by their end users.

Innovation is not just limited to relatively basic, mechanical items within the developing world. Of course in the remote villages that we service there is no electricity but in cities such as Kampala many people have mobile phones. We typically turnover our smartphones every 2 years in the developed world. This is because the battery gradually degrades over time and becomes such that we cannot take it anywhere without also taking a charger with us. Not so in Uganda. There are a number of telephone shops that will gladly work with you to replace your phone battery and give it a tune-up. Those same shops will also resell old phones to people who can't afford to purchase a new one. I know that we have similar stores in Australia that help us out with the odd repair but I don't know a single person that has bought a second hand phone from a store and I suspect that it's a service that's not even available. I'm not about to argue that Kampala, Uganda is a global hub for IT but I bet there are a certain skills that are more prevalent there than in other, more developed parts of the world.

Fostering innovation in the workplace

As leaders, how do we foster the kind of innovation and creativity in our people that we clearly see in the developing world? If necessity is the mother of all invention then how do we create that necessity in our people? I think that part of the answer is in using the SPORT task assignment model that we explained earlier in the book. When you assign a task to one of your people do you show them how to go about completing the task as part of your instructions? If you do, then you're probably falling into one of the most common managerial traps that there is… you are effectively doing their work for them. You're taking away the opportunity for them to think for themselves and innovate. You're also robbing yourself of ever being surprised at your employee's creativity.

Allow me to explain. Everyone uses the term "work" in a different way. If you think about it, it's a word we use in a variety of ways. It's a noun when we are using it to describe our "workplace" and it's a verb when we use it to describe the process of "working". At the front-line often "hard work" is rewarded. Additional hours, attention to detail and obedience are often the hallmarks of doing a good job. In more senior roles the concept of "working smart not hard" tends to emerge. People are remunerated for making the right decisions and that is often what characterises a good job in such roles. I would argue that in order for your people to feel liberated, empowered and motivated you need to do more than just assign tasks without dictating "how" they might go about it. You also need to define the very concept of work and "a good job" in such a way that it encourages discretion and autonomy at all levels of your organisation. The reality is that your front-line workforce will almost always be aware of a number of different opportunities for improvement. They are your single best source of intelligence about the company and in most instances are vastly untapped resources. Your people already know the answers. They are no less creative and innovative than those people I've met in the developing world. It's just that you are probably defining their job in such a way that they think you don't want them to think.

As the world becomes an increasingly global market-place, barriers to entry internationally are being torn down. This is especially the case in the services industry where anyone with access to the internet can now compete with you. Websites like upwork.com, freelancer.com.au and guru.com have all been designed to make it as easy as possible for people all around the world to engage the best people for the job, irrespective of their physical location. The reality is that if you are trying to compete and succeed in such a global marketplace then innovation is key. It's something that comes so naturally to people in the developing world but unless you actively seek to promote innovation and creativity within your work-team it's inevitable that you will be left behind.

Chapter 10 – Key Insights

- Innovation is often borne out of genuine need.
- Leaders should NOT focus on HOW to go about each task they assign if they want their people to come up with innovative approaches and ideas.
- We all have the potential for creativity and innovation but we will only invest our hearts and minds in this pursuit if leaders create the kind of environment where this is encouraged, celebrated and necessary.

Chapter 11: Measuring Value

One of the first things that struck me about Africa was the overwhelming fertility of the land. As I flew into Entebbe for the first time I was overwhelmed with the bright green crops, beautiful lakes and relatively sparse population. It might sound like a strange thing to notice but I come from one of the driest continents on the planet and nowadays it seems that we are almost constantly in drought. I guess I just assumed from all of the commercials on television that Africa was a dusty, horrible place and I couldn't have been further from the truth.

The first thing that we did when we arrived at the village of Katoma was go and visit a local leader with in the community, Pastor Caleb. Caleb is an amazing man with one of the deepest voices and broadest smiles that I've ever encountered but it wasn't either of those things that struck me first about his home. As we drove down the drive-way and pulled over to the left, the first thing I saw as I got out was a beautiful looking Mango tree. Mangoes are my favourite fruit and I had a tree when I was a kid. I was immediately jealous, and as I turned right and looked up, there in front of me was one of the biggest avocado tries that I'd ever seen. Back home, it's not uncommon for one mango to be worth $5 and avocados are almost always somewhere between $3 and $4 depending on the time of year. In Uganda they seem to grow everywhere.

As we sat for a meal with Caleb and his family later on that day he brought out the most flavoursome papaya that I've ever eaten - with the quality of fruit that you can only get in the tropics. It was delicious and I was intrigued by the price of what we were eating. Caleb laughed and informed me that everything we were eating was grown in his backyard. The potatoes, beans, papaya – all of it was grown by their family. I was still intrigued and was keen to find out what the value of various fruits and vegetables were in Uganda. The first thing that I learnt was that the value of various fruits and vegetables is relatively flexible and that most of the time families will barter and share various different foods with each other. If they did have to go to the market to purchase something extra then they would pay with the local shillings. 1000 shillings works out to be about 30 cents Australian. With 1000 shillings you could get 2 bags of onions or even more Avocados. I'm not sure why onions are more expensive than Avocados in the village that I visited but they are and it really emphasised to me how flexible (even notional) the price of various foods that we take for granted back home really is. It's not connected so intrinsically with the qualities of the soil, weather and choices that local families make about what to plant in their vegetable patch. Value in the developing world is determined by the same forces of supply and demand, but there are far more variables at play than just the choices that Caleb and his neighbours make when planting their crops.

In Australia, together with our local produce, we might buy asparagus from Peru, garlic from China and peaches from California. That amazing global supply chain comes at a cost. So too do all of the guys negotiating big global deals. Then there's the local farmers in Australia who are trying to ply the case for local production. There might even be the dilemma when you go to buy something of whether to buy a name brand or generic supermarket brand. It's a complicated business.

It's genuinely hard for me to determine which system is better. It's hard to argue with the cost and simplicity of Caleb's papaya and avocado. However, the choice and convenience of the local supermarket has its real benefits. Or does it?

As I ponder the concept of "value" in Uganda I can't stop thinking about Caleb laughing at me. Of course he was very proud of how productive his garden was. However, his laughter was also driven because the questions I was asking were not really relevant to him. You see I visited with Pastor Caleb every day for a week and even at the end of that time I was not 100% clear who lived with him, who he considered family and who might just be visiting. My sense is the cultural norms of sharing and seeing your fellow villagers as an extended part of the family is very strong. So much so that when two neighbours "barter" for different foods the concept of price just isn't relevant. Maybe Caleb will share a meal with a neighbour today, maybe they will visit with him tomorrow. Nobody is keeping records as the strong sense of community that they all share is able to transcend individual greed.

Whenever we distribute a water filtration system in Uganda we also ask how many household members that family has. It's good for us to know the impact that each filter will have but it is also useful to be able to explain how more encompassing the concept of family is over there. The average household that we distribute our water filtration systems to has 10 family members. That might include 3 generations of people. It might include parents and newly-weds all within the same 1 or 2 room building. It's truly mind boggling for people who come from a more individualistic culture. We simply can't comprehend it. The best way to describe it is that they simply value different things. They don't value maximising the price of their vegetables nearly as much as they do having a close family. Another thing that struck me was how quickly I was welcomed into people's homes. I genuinely felt like a member of their family and that's why I talk with such confidence about the more inclusive concept of a family unit in Uganda.

As mentioned in Chapter 4, on my final day in Katoma we didn't have much time left and were very worried but that didn't mean that we were able to skip our morning visit to the pastor's house to visit his family before going down the road. There are a few social rules that are very important to follow over here. I'm not 100% clear on all of the rules but I think that we mainly needed to visit the pastor's house on the way to the village each day because he was hosting us in the community. That visit was usually relatively short. Another rule was that we always needed to eat a meal with the pastor's family before leaving. In a way I don't think that this rule was applicable to us – more to them. It would have been dishonourable for them in some way for us not to share a meal with them. It would have reflected poorly on them not us. Interestingly, it didn't matter how late we were running both of these two stop offs had to happen each day. This would become a problem later in the day when we were running very late. Our taxi driver was actually already waiting at our agreed meeting point and we were at least 1 hour away. In the morning we had explained to the Pastor that we would NOT be able to stop off on the way back. He seemed to agree but then when the time actually came he told us that his wife had laid out food and she would be very upset if we didn't eat it.

This was an awkward meeting of cultures that's for sure. It felt a bit rude to me because it seemed like it was a bit selfish to insist on a meal that would mean that both the guests of that meal and the driver already waiting on a road side 1 hour away would be inconvenienced. However, that's when it was pointed out to me that the guy waiting for us probably wouldn't be upset at all. It was just the way things were here. That was a real paradigm shift for me. When I thought about it, within that context, the only reason I was frustrated was that someone waiting for an hour WOULD be frustrated about waiting... when I realised that was NOT the case these cultural norms made sense all of a sudden.

I've had similar paradigm shifting experiences in Cambodia. On my first visit to the rehabilitation centre I was a little shocked to see how well set-up they were to produce all manner of different disability aides for their patients. One of the things I was shocked to find was an entire production lines for hands. This hadn't been disclosed to me in any of our numerous planning sessions so I was actually a tiny bit frustrated. Having said that, I kept my emotions in check and was open to learning.

During my first tour of the "hand making" factory I realised that the end product was very visually impressive but was not particularly functional. It looked great and is what I would call a "cosmetic prosthetic". It had embedded nails and what looked like veins inbuilt into the moulds however below the surface the fingers were only held stiff with coat-hanger wire and once

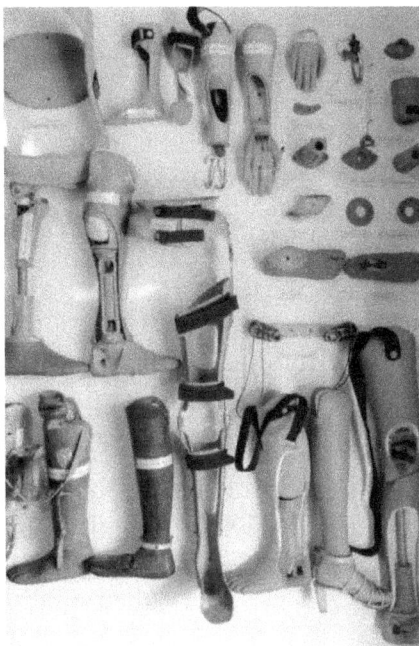

Various devices available from the rehabilitation centre that I visited in Cambodia

these fingers were bent more than once or twice they had a propensity to either loosen entirely or break. On the up-side what I quickly realised was that this hand simply screwed onto the prosthetic arms that they were making for people. Our hand also has a screw so there was no problem with giving recipients both of the hands as they might each be useful in different context.

I thought that this idea was fantastic and was excited to share the news with the rehabilitation centre Manager however was greeted with slightly less enthusiasm. He kept on talking about cost and wages for his staff and I didn't understand. We had both

131

talked about the fact that our hands always need to be distributed free of charge and that we can't pay any bribes or inducements whatsoever. It felt like we were back to square one again. Then I tried to listen really closely (as best as you can with a translator) one last time and I heard something different.

You see that centre was funded at that time entirely from USAID and AUSAID. It was a kind of loose joint venture between the USA and Australian governments that had been in place since the Vietnam war but both governments had announced plans to begin to scale back their funding. FINALLY, I realised what he was saying. He wasn't asking for a bribe he was just expressing a real concern that his five men that were employed to make prosthetics were at risk of losing their job and if I gave them hands for free that was threatening to them.

Once again, this was challenging for me but in a different way. On one level this was still sounding a bit like corruption. That's probably what we would call it in Australia. However, on another level I could see that this man was still trying to look after people that were not well-off men. Some of the prosthetics technicians that were working at that rehabilitation centre had disabilities themselves and all of them came from relatively poor communities. I found myself challenged because I could see that employing these men was potentially wasteful yet I could also see that there were five people with good jobs that they could be proud of. Each of those five people had families and they were the primary wage-earner. In the developing world small problems can become life and death struggles quickly and the reality is that losing a job for any of these men might have had tragic consequences.

My visits to both Uganda and Cambodia have made me more grounded as a person. The jobs people are doing seem tangible. The values they place on various goods are more closely aligned to supply and demand. On top of that the value of friendship and relationship is much greater. The importance that is placed on family and on supporting the rest of the community is significant. The value that is placed on these people-related variables resonates with me. It doesn't just impress me because it's a nice feel-good thing to say. It impresses me because I can see clearly how important having a close community can be in both environments. There are tangible benefits for both cultures valuing people highly.

The Rise of Corporate Social Responsibility

It seems to me that we might have lost our way a bit in the Western World and in business generally. The values we place on things are always measured in dollars and cents. Yet the way we then determine what something is worth is so far removed from the productive fabric of our society that it's completely conceivable we could all apparently get "richer" whilst concurrently seeing our societies fall apart.

I think this risk is most visible within the commercial world. The first businesses were cooperatives. They were farmers who banded together and formed alliances to ensure that as a whole they were better off. The benefit of such organisations was unquestionable.

The community was clearly better off as a result of those organisations being established. In recent years I believe we have witnessed a bit of a trend of "what's old is new again". Corporations all around the world are beginning to be asked about whether they have "socially conscious investments" and how much of their profits are reinvested or donated within the local community. Almost all large organisations now have a Corporate Social Responsibility policy together with a small team of employees focussed on just that area of accountability. Some countries (like the United Kingdom) are even legislating that this companies consider the social impact of their decisions on the local communities within which they operate.

The trend towards recognising social value within the workplace is showing no sign of abating. Leaders in the modern world need to be open to valuing decisions in a more holistic sense. Not only is this good news for communities it's good news for workplaces. When the value that companies place on various initiatives reflects the true benefit to the community and not a notional cash value I think that the company is providing employees with something that they can get passionate about.

Investment Evaluation

I don't know about you but a really great Net Payback Period or Net Present Value really doesn't excite me that much. They are important numbers that need to be calculated when you are making an investment decision but financial measures should only be one component of a leader's thought process. Did you know that about half of all mergers and acquisitions fail? That's right, every year, literally trillions of dollars are invested in business deals that ultimately fail. These deals are not put together by idiots. Often the deals are conceived by some of the smartest people of our generation. When a board approves spending billions of dollars on one single deal then they want to be sure that it's been thought through really carefully. So not only will several incredibly intelligent people have come up with the idea and brokered an "in principle" agreement to proceed, boards will almost always commission what are called "due diligence" investigations into the proposed transaction. Due Diligence is a complicated thing to explain in one sentence but just imagine that the best most expensive lawyers, accountants and IT professionals are all asked to audit a proposed transaction from top to bottom. Its serious stuff and people with large reputations are each putting their name on the deal before it proceeds. So, if all that capability and money are thrown at a transaction how could half of all transactions possibly fail?

Typically, we are told that most proposed acquisitions simply fail because of people-related issues. You see, really smart people pushing paper around on a table simply does not replicate all of the million different moving parts that make up a successful enterprise. I'm invited to conduct Human Resources Due Diligence several times each year. It's the core of my consulting business. Typically, I'm engaged to investigate the kinds of transactions where there are lots of people involved and someone has identified that "people might be an issue here". We are very good at our job and typically identify a range of important issues to consider as part of the transaction. However, it never ceases to amaze me the number of transactions that proceed without someone like me looking at the people-related implications of the transaction.

I don't care if a business employs one person or a 100,000 there are ALWAYs important people-related considerations to be made. The less people involved, the more important it is to assess what their likely motivation will be like after the transaction has finished. The more people involved, the more complexity that might exist in labour laws, industrial instruments and payroll matters. Either way, it's entirely possible to predict many of the people-related challenges that occur when mergers and acquisitions fail, it's just that sadly most companies don't value this part of the transaction as highly as they do the financial or legal aspects.

On face value, the nature of business and investment evaluation in general is far more sophisticated than a simply barter system in a subsistence farming community. It's hard to argue with the documentation and complexity that two dozen of the world's smartest consultants can conjure up to support the need for a big transaction proceeding and earning everyone lots of money. It's also hard not to wonder whether in all that complexity we sometimes lose touch with what really matters. The further abstracted our valuation is from something we make with our hands or grow in the soil, the more room for error there is. It doesn't mean that we should stop tackling big, complex problems. I just think that in business we sometimes allow the complexity to blind us from identifying the critical issues in big decisions – especially when those issues are people-related.

Chapter 11 – Key Insights
- "Value" is not strictly a financial concept - Often non-financial dimensions of value are more important under certain circumstances. - Inspired workplaces consider all aspects of value creation when evaluating investment decisions.

Chapter 12: Sustainability

As I've previously mentioned, one of the trips that I will never forget was my visit to a refugee camp in Uganda. To recap, this was not a place where people were fleeing Uganda (one of the poorest countries in the world), this camp was for people who were fleeing from Rwanda or the Democratic Republic of Congo to the relative safety of Uganda. It was an incredibly challenging trip because here in Australia there is so much media coverage about "illegal immigrants" and "queue jumpers" that you can't help but have slightly biased views about refugee camps. One of the most striking thing to me was that this refugee camp had no fences. It wasn't a situation of people being detained while they waited to be processed. In fact, people referred to the camp as a "refugee settlement camp". People had effectively chosen to live there because of the plentiful crops that were available in nearby fields (provided by the United Nations and Ugandan government).

During the trip it was so much fun taking photos of the kids. Fun not just because these kids were beautiful and happy but because they would all shriek with laughter when they saw the photos of themselves on my digital screen. It was the first time most of these kids had seen a digital camera let alone seen themselves on that screen. Watching their faces light up was addictive and I took many of my photos purely for their benefit. Out of the corner of my eye I saw one of the kids dragging a toy along behind him with a piece of string. I looked carefully and could see that this ingenious little kid had effectively made a toy car out of old plastic bottles. As he got closer he picked it up and showed me his most prized possession. It was a special moment and I took a photo.

Later, as we were leaving the refugee camp I climbed into our car and my feet brushed aside the plastic bottles we'd been saving up on the floor of a vehicle. It instantly reminded me of that kid who had made a toy car out of plastic bottles and I felt like other kids might like some of my old bottles. We had 6 empty bottles altogether and as I began to hand them out what happened brought me to tears immediately. The kids (still happy) were desperate to get their hands on those bottles and a couple of young boys got into a semi-serious fight over one of them.

They were fighting over my rubbish...

A boy with a toy car

I wasn't able to stop crying at this point but tried my best to hold it together while we waved goodbye to the kids. As we drove off I was silent for a long time. I didn't value those plastic bottles. To me, they were irritating throughout our journey taking up space in the car and if we came across a rubbish bin I would have likely thrown them away the second I got the chance. Yet here were a group of human beings that were genuinely desperate to have my rubbish.

I think that the contrast between the way we live in the developing world and the way the rest of the world lives is always just as striking as that plastic bottle example. If these people were living in our own backyards we simply wouldn't be able to justify our behaviour. We wouldn't accept throwing out half of the things that we throw in our rubbish bins. The fact is that these people don't generally live in our backyard. They live on the other side of the world and it might as well be an entirely different planet because most of us never get an opportunity to visit these people, let alone become friends with them.

A broader concept of sustainability

Of course the term "sustainability" encapsulates much more than just environmental issues. To adopt a sustainable approach in the workplace means that you're not just thinking about the short-term, but you're investing in an approach that will generate value for many years into the future. At its most extreme, a sustainable approach means building a business that is built to last rather than managing based on share-price fluctuations.

When we consider sustainability more broadly I think it has far-reaching implications from a people perspective. If we are to manage people in such a way that they generate value for our business in the long-term then that means investing in learning and development, in building the capacity of each and every employee so that the productivity of your business also grows exponentially. It means investing in employee engagement. Every dollar you invest in ensuring that you have an engaged workforce that is emotionally connected to your purpose as a business is well spent because of reduced turnover, absenteeism and ultimately lower wage demands. Employees that are happier and truly motivated in the workplace not only work harder in the short-term but they stick it out when times are tough and remain loyal for longer.

All of those statements might seem obvious; common-sense even. However, I believe this is one of those cases where common sense is remarkably uncommon. Typically when I talk about employee engagement within the workplace the first thing people think of is their annual staff survey. In business, you often get what you measure. So establishing a regular employee engagement survey is really important if you want to signal to your managers that this is an important concept. However, let's be clear, if all you do is ask your employees what they think of you, then you never actually invest in doing something as a result of what they tell you, their engagement is likely to reduce, not increase. You see, if you ask someone what they think, you're also communicating to them that you will consider their views. If you shared your views and were passionate about the opinions you shared, how would you feel if someone considered them, then chose to not act? You don't need to be a psychologist to predict the likely outcome.

Investing in employee engagement

Being serious about building a sustainable workplace requires us to genuinely invest in employee engagement. That means being clear about our purpose as a business. Explaining that to each of our employees clearly when they join company, making sure that their personal purpose in life is aligned to that of your company's, that they share similar beliefs. It means that once those employees commence, ensuring that you make good on your promise. It means ensuring that the way you design roles and divide work enables each person to feel like their contribution is valued, and that they are engaged in meaningful, challenging work where they are encouraged to use their discretion. It's difficult work to construct a scalable workplace like that but if we're serious about ensuring that our human resources are engaged in a sustainable fashion there's no short-cut.

Wondering if you're investing sufficiently in building a sustainable workforce? Of course there is no right or wrong answer to this but if you're looking through your annual budget and cannot see any line items relating to people (aside from wages and on-costs) then it's a good indication that you are currently insufficiently investing in this area. A recent study in the UK found that training investment across all industries was, on average, 2% of turnover. Only one in five employers under-invested by spending 0.5% or less of turnover in this area. Of course every company is different and training is certainly not the "be all and end all" of employee engagement. However, as an objective measure that is comparable across industries, I find the training budget is a good insight to whether each company is really serious about a sustainable workforce. Should each company be aiming to spend at least the average of 2% of turnover? Not necessarily. If you know that you've historically under-invested in this area and have a disengaged or under-skilled workforce then perhaps aiming for more than 2% would be a more realistic goal. Feeling like you just need to defend the status quo? Then perhaps maintaining 2% is an ideal figure.

Chapter 12 – Key Insights

- The future of our planet depends on a more sustainable approach. Inspired cultures value sustainability in all aspects of what they do.
- Sustainability is more than a strictly environmental concern.
- Having a truly sustainable workplace requires us to invest in our people.
- Truly engaged employees are more productive and save money for the workplace in the long-term.

III.   BEING AN INSPIRED LEADER

I first began running my own company and working for myself almost 10 years ago now. As part of my role leading a team, consulting with workplace leaders, providing advice and influencing others has always been a big part of my remit. It's fair to say that I have seen myself as a leader for a long time. I therefore didn't expect that whilst doing aide work in the developing world my concept of what makes a good leader would change forever.

The insights I am sharing in this section are not intended to be a standardised formula for creating the perfect leader. They are simply stories from the developing world that I believe will prompt you to reflect on what makes a great leader and potentially challenge some of your existing preconceptions about the topic.

We start the section by exploring the concept of leadership and explaining the way good managers often sabotage their own evolution as leaders within the business. This section then shares a range of stories that we believe illustrate inspiring leadership characteristics including:

1.   Believing in the worth of all persons
2.   Courage
3.   Grace under pressure
4.   Forgiveness
5.   Generosity
6.   Humanising our goals

Chapter 13: Leadership – a grave responsibility

There are a lot of Chairmen in Uganda. It's a strange title that we use for a completely different purpose in the developed world however over there the title "chairman" is bestowed on a local leader within the community. I was told that there is a form of democratic process sitting behind the election of Chairmen but that this process is somewhat questionable. Apparently it is more of a transitionary structure that's been put in place to replace the former tribal chieftain system. Not being an expert in either current or past structures I can only comment on what I observed of the role of local Chairmen and other leaders in our projects.

Although we only launched the Water Works Program on April 25, 2015 our partners in the UK and Uganda began their preparations for that program several months prior to this. Firstly, they had to establish relationships with local community leaders and representatives to ensure that each village we worked with genuinely wanted our assistance. Then they worked to conduct a census of each village. They collected records of each household, school and medical centre that needed our help and began to tally up how many water systems each village would need. In parallel to this, they began to recruit local youths that might be interested in being involved in such a project as a development and learning activity.

All of this was done before we had sold a single Water Works Program or arranged to ship any of the materials required for distribution over to Uganda.

Each time we distribute water to an entire village it is a major project and takes several days to implement successfully. We typically have two local leaders run the training sessions and coordinate all volunteers. Additionally, we require at least 10 local volunteers that have some pre-training. These local volunteers usually take the lead on the registration process and also marshalling people through the process. All people, both local leaders and volunteers are from the local community or at least neighbouring townships and as such are fluent in local languages and dialects. The success of our project so far has therefore been largely due to working very closely with the local community. As the founder of the initiative I have had very little to do with distribution work except to watch and learn myself. When I'm personally in the field I do not see myself as "leading" the project in any way. I just see myself as the guy that coordinated funding for it. It's a different mindset to what we might expect in the developed world however it's a critical mindset for success with such a project.

I think that one of the universal truths about effective charity work is that if you do not have the support and involvement of the local community then you might as well not bother. Although foreign aid and other charity projects almost always commence with the best of intentions they can never assume that they are beyond reproach or that the local people should accept that generosity without question. Furthermore, cultural nuances and subtle translation difficulties can easily lead to either flawed design or undermine the effective implementation of such efforts. Of course genuine engagement with the local community prior to commencing a new charity project is essential. It might be expensive at times and it will always delay the implementation of such a project but this is a critical next step.

Before we commence distributing the water filtration systems, we typically have a range of guest speakers. I am normally one of those speakers but I only talk very briefly with the help of a translator. The other speakers typically comprise of local government ministers, departmental officials and chairmen from the community. It is clear from the attention that the local community pays to such people that their views are trusted and depended on. In a local village with no access to television, radio or newspapers, local leaders are critical to give people a sense of hope and confidence that they are making good decisions. As the township grows and some of these poorer countries in the world become more developed some of those decisions will in fact become extremely significant.

Determining whether to fight or agree with relocation of households for various government projects and consulting about the ideal location of new infrastructure, roads, water wells and trade-centres are examples of decisions that the communities we work within are likely to need to make in the future. The implications of each of these decisions, if poor, could be dire for these small vulnerable communities. As such, the importance of each of these communities having strong local leadership is critical as they grow. They need to know that they have strong leaders who are willing to fight for the issues that matter to others.

It is fair to say that attendees of the Mega Limb camp in Bangalore India also appear to hold leaders in an equally high regard as what I observed in Uganda. It is fair to say that the relatively stratified culture in India might contribute to this. In actual fact, those vulnerable people in India might not have much say in who their leaders are. However, that doesn't make them any less dependent on the decisions that they make. Leadership is in fact a grave responsibility in all parts of the world but this is especially evident within the developing world.

A good friend of mine once suggested to me that money doesn't buy happiness, it just gives you freedom to make some more choices that weren't available to you prior. A common theme of this book has been the notion that there is very little that differentiates between the haves and have-nots of the world. We are each emotionally, spiritually and intellectually equal when born. Tragically, some of us just have a greater ability to self-determinate. In the world that we live in, those of us with material wealth simply have more choices available to us. The irony of this is that having travelled extensively in the developed world many of the people with the most choices available appear to be the least happy. Those of us that have the greatest ability to make a difference in the world from a financial perspective so often choose the easy way out and fail to step into our own destiny in that regard.

The role of a leader is actually a very simple concept. Essentially, you are a leader if you are able to influence the actions of others. If people either look to you for advice or guidance or emulate your actions in any way then you ARE a leader whether you like it or not. In fact, I would go as far as to say that each and every one of us influences others in one way or another. We might not take on a leadership role in every situation however we each take on a leadership role under the right circumstances. I don't care whether you have the words "Vice President" or "Manager" in your job title. Each and every one of us has the ability to take on a leadership role on issues that matter.

Leadership in the developed world is no less important than in those small vulnerable villages that I've described in this book. The only difference as I can see it is that more choices are available to us. If you have won the birthplace lottery and happen to live in an amazing place like Australia, the USA, Canada or the UK then options abound. We are SO lucky to live in the places that we do and we almost have infinite choices available to us. Not only does each leader have the ability to change the course of the world but I believe every single one of us has the ability to take on a leadership role in the world.

If you are reading this book it's likely that you have already recognised that we each have an ability to make a big difference in the world. It's probably one of the things that attracted you to this book. Now that you recognise your potential role as a leader I ask you to dive deeper. As you read the following chapters in this book there are a number of different leadership lessons that could potentially supercharge your development as a leader. Please take this book as an opportunity to make a commitment to yourself that YOU are going to be the leader that you were put on this planet to be. YOU are going to be the change that you want to see in the world. YOU are going to take others along that journey with you. If each person who reads this book has the courage to make that choice we could send a serious shock-wave of influence throughout the world. The time to make the choice is now. Please take that first step with me.

Sabotaging your own leadership journey

If you're like me you have always known that you have the potential to be a great leader. Maybe someone told you that once when you were a kid. Maybe you've just always had that ability to influence the group. Maybe you were just always an independent thinker and weren't easily swayed by others.

Of course recognizing that you have potential to be a leader is a different thing to having the courage to attempt to do so. I think that a lot of courage is required to be a leader because it means confronting any fear that we have of failure. Marianne Williamson said in best in 1992 when she first coined one of the most commonly referenced quotes today:

> *"Our deepest fear is not that we are inadequate. Our deepest fear is that we are powerful beyond measure. It is our light, not our darkness that most frightens us.' We ask ourselves, Who am I to be brilliant, gorgeous, talented, fabulous? Actually, who are you not to be? ..."*

The thing that holds most of us back from being the leader we were born to be is actually a fear of failure. We're afraid to admit to ourselves that we were put on this planet to be nothing less than a rock star. Yet, over the course of our life-time we typically let little things beat us down and over time eventually convince ourselves that we are meant to just be ordinary. It couldn't be further from the truth.

We are all born potential leaders. The sad fact is that many of us sabotage our own journey before it even begins. One of the secrets to being a leader in the modern world is accepting that you do not need to be perfect. We all have strengths and weaknesses. Chances are that some of those strengths are what has got you into a leadership role. The scary thing is that as your leadership journey evolves, it can often be those very strengths that derail your development as a leader.

Although derailment can sometimes occur with more established leaders, research suggests that it's a more typical challenge for new or emerging leaders. While derailment occurs for different reasons for each impacted individual, research has identified the four most common symptoms:

1. Poor Interpersonal relationships

2. Failing to meet business objectives

3. Difficulty adapting to new circumstances

4. Failure to build an effective team

When does it occur?

Some experts in the field have estimated that up to 25% of high-potential leaders experience derailment, and that most of us have the potential to derail at some point in time. So when should we be on the look-out? The most common situations within the workplace appear to be as follows:

- Creating new ventures and business opportunities

- Managing change and innovation

- Dealing with acquisitions and mergers

- Addressing competitive issues and pressures

These are all high pressure situations where it is easy to become absorbed (even obsessed) with the work that you are doing; losing perspective in relation to anything or anyone else. In addition, in each of these situations, there are a number of external factors influencing the outcome of the work. This results in the individual concerned being less likely to feel "in control" of their own circumstances.

What can we do about it?

It is important to identify derailment early before it spirals out of control. This can sometimes be a very challenging thing to do. In my practice as a Psychologist, I've often found that leadership derailment occurs as the result of an "over-played" strength. Maybe you've always been very detail focused. It's something that you're proud of and it's something that has helped propel into a leadership position with your peers. Under pressure it's only natural to depend a lot on those tried and tested strengths however there are plenty of circumstances where detail focus can actually become more of a hindrance than a help. All of a sudden that detail focused leader is beginning to derail and what are they likely to do? Depend even MORE on the very personality trait that is undermining their success in the first place.

We all need trusted confidants and mentors. People who will encourage us in good times and bad. Having a trusted confidant is critical to avoiding derailment as a leader because it is much more likely that those people who care about us will be amongst the first people to identify the problem. In all likelihood it will NOT be you that identifies this first. Just because you have decided to step-up into your destiny as a leader it doesn't mean that your journey must be a solitary one. I believe that as we each take that first step or two during our leadership journey one of the very first steps that we each need to take is to share more with our mentors, friends and family. Those are the people that love you and want you to succeed but unless you share what's going on in your life they simply don't have enough information to help.

Chapter 13 – Key Insights

- Leadership is equally critical in the modern workplace as it is in the developing world.
- We are all potential leaders just waiting to step-up into our destiny.
- Many of us sabotage our leadership journey before it even gets started by letting the fear of failure take hold.
- Good leaders can often derail by "over-playing" the strengths that got them to where they are at in the first place.
- Great leaders surround themselves with trusted mentors and loved ones and are open to feedback from those very people.

Chapter 14: The worth of all persons

During late 2013 I was lucky enough to have an opportunity to travel to Phnom Penh, Cambodia. It's the capital of Cambodia and just like many other capital cities in the developing world it's relatively cosmopolitan. I was staying in a very clean and comfortable hotel within a safe neighbourhood in the city and each morning we would travel a short distance to a rehabilitation centre where we were fitting our prosthetics to people in the need.

On my first night in Phnom Penh I wasn't quite brave enough to travel very far from my hotel and went across the street to a local restaurant to eat dinner. At that stage I hadn't had a chance to get my bearings and felt like staying in a tourist region might be a good idea for my first night. The meal was fantastic and as I was mid-way through the single most flavoursome chicken curry that I have ever had in my life I was interrupted by a small child who came through the restaurant selling friendship bracelets. I purchased one of the bracelets with some small change that I had in my pocket and went back to my meal.

The next day, on the way to the rehabilitation centre, I asked my interpreter about the little girl from the night before. I was concerned about the safety of this small girl walking around selling bracelets so late at night by herself and I also didn't really understand whether it was something I should have been encouraging. My question came from a place of genuine ignorance and I felt like I needed some advice about whether or not I should support such activities. My interpreter explained that often using the children was a much easier way for the parents to sell their wares. He explained that there was a chance that child's parent was close-by and so the safety of the child might not have been in question. He then lowered his voice and explained that at times children work for other people besides their parents. At times many children would be working for the one person and this would help that person become quite wealthy at the expense of the children.

Of course when I had purchased that bracelet I felt like I was doing the equivalent of supporting a local kid's lemonade stand out the front of their house. A fun game for the kids that they were not obligated to take part in. Based on my interpreter's advice it sounded like my actions had at best supported child labour and at worst potentially slavery. My heart broke at listening to this story. I was a bit disappointed at my own naivety the night before however I was also struck with the futility of the situation. If that little girl could make $10 more for her family each night than her mother could make on her own then maybe it wasn't so bad. On a case-by-case or day-to-day basis maybe these actions are justified. However as one day becomes a second and third, eventually a little girl's childhood is at best transformed and at worst stolen from her altogether.

I personally grew up in an incredibly loving family environment. I was also lucky enough to have my most fundamental needs met like food, shelter, clean water or security. I am the first to admit that I absolutely took all of that for granted at the time and it's almost impossible for me to imagine the life of that little girl I bought a bracelet from. What I do know is that if she needs to work regularly as a child she will likely have less time to get a good education. I know that she is growing up in a country where access to educational opportunities are slim to start with. I know that she's growing up in a country where she will be expected to live 10 less years than someone in Australia. So I know that through no fault of her own her life will be more difficult for her than it was for me.

I don't pretend to be able to understand what that little girl thinks about her life and the world in general. However, I do know that she and I have very few genetic differences. We have more things in common than the things that separate us. It's just the material things really that make us different. She was born with dreams and hopes every bit as big as mine. Maybe she wants to be famous. Maybe she wants to be a police-woman or IT professional. Maybe she wants to be a world leader. Either way I know that I don't deserve to be able to realise my dreams any more than her. I believe she's been put on this earth for a purpose; that there's a plan for her and although it might not happen today or tomorrow, one day in the future I believe she'll find that purpose. Like I said in chapter one – I truly believe that we're all born to be rock stars... that little bracelet vendor is no different.

If that story of the little girl didn't resonate for you then please allow me to present another quandary for your consideration. If you've travelled much in the developing world you will often note the stark contrast between the glistening new high-rise office towers and the shanty-towns and deteriorating old buildings that often sit adjacent to those newer buildings. As a whole, most nations encourage investment and responsible development. They know that with every large building construction project there are thousands of jobs created and that sends financial ripples through the community. Once built, often that new building can attract new companies to base themselves in that country that otherwise would not have been open to the idea and once again, positive ripples are sent through the community. As a whole, the nation becomes wealthier and the developing nation becomes a little bit more developed piece by piece.

If you've done much travelling in the developing world, you'll have come across the concept of the "new city". I first encountered this concept in Cambodia. Effectively, the government had made a planning decision to relocate the commercial centre of their city. This would called the "new city" and as you drove past that part of the town you could see literally hundreds of buildings being constructed. The speed with which such initiatives can be attempted in the developing world is sometimes astonishing. The impact of development on such a scale is unquestionably powerful and has the potential to financially transform an entire country. However, such progress comes at a huge social cost.

If the government rezones a parcel of land that you happen to live on in Australia or the Western world, normally this would result in your net-wealth increasing dramatically. Pretty quickly the developers would come knocking offering staggering amounts of money to buy your humble home. As a result, you walk away a wealthy person who is potentially able to buy an even better home somewhere else. If you live in the developing world the chances are that you don't have any formal title or deed over the parcel of land that you live on. Maybe the community owns the land, maybe you've legally been squatting on someone else's land for all of this time. Either way, the relocation of shanty towns and other inhabitants to make way for the "new city" tends to be justified on the basis of the greater good for the community. However, if I ask you adopt the perspective of someone being asked to relocate with no recompense or assistance then the story becomes far more equivocal. Does the 5 year old child that was born into this situation and currently lives in one of those shanties deserve to have hopes and dreams? I'm pretty sure that all readers would agree on the answer to that question.

One of the things that I firmly believe is that we are all essentially the same. Rich or poor, gay or straight, male or female, our basic make-up is the same. The thing that makes us human is the same. One of my mentors, an incredible business leader and consultant called Justin O'Connell once said to me that "at the root of all discrimination is a belief of inequity." He was explaining this in the context of a large organisational change we were working on together and we were debating some of the fundamental principles required to design a sustainable structure moving forward. That basic principle, initially revealed in the context of an organisational design project have become one of my most deeply held beliefs. I think those beliefs were probably there from a very early age but I just didn't realise how significant they were until that discussion with Justin.

In my experience across many workplaces in a variety of different industries there are very few people who believe that they are discriminating against others. We all like to think that we are good people and that we give all of our co-workers are fair chance at succeeding. We like to think that everyone is on a level playing field and that with hard-work and discipline we can all achieve anything. Sadly, that simply isn't true. Three billion people get by each year on less than $2.50 per day. That's almost half of the world's population. A staggering 48% of the world's wealth is controlled by just the top 1% of income earners. Staggeringly, if you can afford to buy this book you're probably one of those people. If you earn an income of more than $32,500 USD per year then you're in the top 1%.

Hopefully some of those statistics put things into perspective for you and help you see just how lucky you are. The reality is that if you are one of the few people that is chosen for a leadership position in a company then you're also in a very privileged position. Of course we could debate whether or not you deserved that promotion more than the next person. We could debate the extent to which you have unique skills and knowledge that made you the obvious choice. Maybe there was no luck involved at all! My point is the debate is unhelpful and it doesn't really matter what the real answer is.

One thing that hopefully we can all agree on is that each and every one of the people you work with is someone's little boy or little girl. They were born with hopes and dreams and a special purpose. Maybe they are actively living that purpose in their role right now. Maybe they are doing incredible things in their spare time. Maybe they overcame overwhelming hardship as a child.

In 1972 Malcolm S. Forbes first shared a quote that is still relevant today:

> *"You can easily judge the character of a man by how he treats those who can do nothing for him."*

It's not possible for us to know the intimate hopes and dreams of every person that we meet but they are still there. Still just as potent as yours. Still just as important as yours. The vast majority of people we meet in our life-time will not be able to "do anything" for us. That means that the vast majority of our interactions with other people are purely character testing moments. How do you treat people in those moments? Are you fixated on your own plans and hopes so much that you find it difficult to treat others with dignity and respect?

To be completely honest I know that I fail this test all the time. I'm extremely driven and as a result I often bulldoze the opinions of others and fail to invest sufficient time in truly listening to others. Of course it's a confronting thing to admit this to yourself. However, I think it's even MORE confronting when I think about the underlying belief that this behaviour reveals. You see each time I've bulldozed the opinions of others I believe it's revealed a subconscious belief that my

161

hopes and dreams are more important than anyone else. As Justin said to me many years ago, that belief of inequality if we fertilise it too much can turn into some pretty nasty stuff. There's a huge social stigma associated with admitting to ourselves that we secretly believe our hopes and dreams are more important than everyone else's. It's something that I struggle to admit to myself let alone anyone else. The problem is that if we keep on burying that belief and pretending it's not there our growth as leaders is always going to be limited.

Truly, the "worth of all persons" is a universal truth. It's a principle that is worth adopting as a member of the human race but it's a critical value for each and every leader to internalise. Until we can value the hopes and dreams of other people equally to our own, we can't possibly hope to influence substantive or sustainable change in others.

Chapter 14 – Key Insights

-   Nobody on the planet is born more important or deserving than anyone else.
-   We are all born to be ROCK STARS.
-   Great leaders treat all people with dignity and respect. They demonstrate that they truly understand the worth of all people.

Chapter 15: Courage

My first trip to Cambodia was a fairly discombobulating experience for me. I had travelled by myself a lot in the past but never into the developing world and rarely had I ever put my complete faith in somebody else. On that first trip I'd been referred to a local tour-guide to help plan my accommodation and transfers. The gentleman I was working with had previously worked with a teacher at the PLC girls' school in Perth. PLC had recently made some hands for Cambodia and had a long track record of coordinating student aide trips to the country so they were kind enough to share their trusted contacts with me. My wife can attest to the fact that I'm normally a very anxious traveller so when I first walked out of the gates at Phnom Penh and started looking for the face of a man I'd never met my senses were on edge. It's not that I don't trust people in general, it's just that I get very worried about leaving the relative safety of a country I know very well for a foreign land that I don't really understand.

Although it was a great relief to meet my guide and be in the car on the way to the hotel I was still on edge during that taxi ride. I had no idea what the accommodation would be like or whether the area I was staying in was safe. Of course I had nothing to worry about but during the trip I was still nervous. When you're in that heightened state of awareness I think you notice a lot more about your surroundings. I saw a family of 4 riding on one motorbike, immediately behind them was another bike with 2 men and an entire air conditioning unit! Talk about a "Toto we're not in Kansas anymore" moment...

Nearing the end of my journey we drove past a building site. Even a building site in the developing world is worth seeing for those of us that have been brought up in the West. There were no petitions to hide the site and keep commuters safe. There were no signs to say that this was a construction zone. As I looked up to the top of the three-story brick building that was being demolished, I could see two different men working with sledge-hammers to knock down the building. They didn't have helmets on or high visibility jackets. In fact, these men were not even wearing shoes that I could tell. That's NOT the most shocking part of what I was looking at. These men were standing 3 stories up, balanced on a double-brick wall and it was the very same wall that they were trying to demolish with a sledge-hammer.

Being Australian, we grow up hearing stories about how amazing a feat it was to build the Sydney Harbour Bridge, that 2,500 people worked on that project and it took 9 years to build. There were 15 deaths during construction . Sadly, construction in those days was a deadly game. Sadly, construction in the developing world is STILL a deadly game. I find it so sad that anyone needs to risk their life at work. Aside from people who work in the defence industry, I don't think that there is any job that is important enough to die for and one of the gravest responsibilities a leader has is to ensure that their employees go home in the same state that they arrived that morning.

When I arrived at the rehabilitation centre on that first day I have to say that I was a little underwhelmed. This trip had been months in the making and I had a list of 50 people who were in need of hands. When I arrived there were only 5 people waiting. It's always notoriously difficult to arrange Helping Hands distribution trips. That's why we typically rely on our charity partner, the Ellen Meadows Prosthetic Hands Foundation to distribute most of the hands we make. Liaising with someone in their second language via a combination of email and telephone is not easy and of course you're dealing with such delicate subject matter that it's very easy to offend people if you're too forthright in your requests. So although helping 5 people was something that I could easily get excited

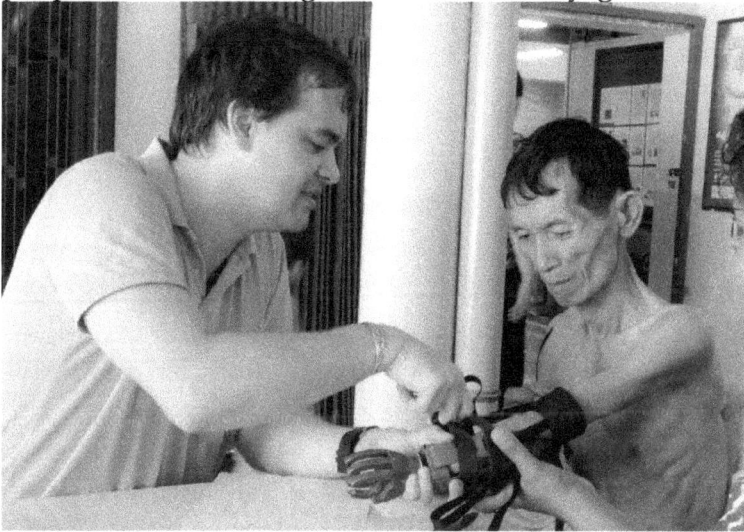

Man being fitted with a hand

about I was also a little bit deflated and worried that somehow we had our wires crossed during communications.

Of course we went on to fit all 5 people with hands. Two of those people were double amputees so we actually fit 7 hands that day in total and I then decided to talk to the director of the rehabilitation centre about why there were so few people in attendance. He explained that because it was the wet season and the day was slightly overcast many people would have been too scared to venture out of their homes. When I pointed out that we had a four wheel drive vehicle and could go and visit them he explained that monsoonal rains could quickly make roads impassable, even for our vehicle. He then

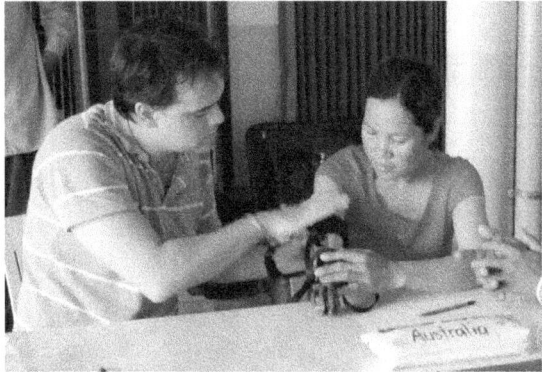

Woman being fitted with a hand

explained that many people who were in need of our hands were planning on travelling all day to receive this gift. It was going to be a significant journey and most of them would have to pay for their own transportation. He said that it would cost about $10 USD for the round trip on the back of a motorbike taxi (called "Moto" in Cambodia) and that amount would be close to a month's wages for some of these people.

All of a sudden the picture he was painting become clear to me. Here I was, flying into one of the poorest countries in the world, working with some of the most vulnerable people within that country but I was still characterising their situation as if they had all of the same options that I did. Effectively each of my hand recipients was going to need to outlay a significant amount of money to travel to our centre, they were going to need to commit an entire day for the round-trip. On top of all of that they were also going to have to run the risk that if it rained they might be stranded in a monsoon; a situation that could become deadly for some of these people very quickly.

In that moment my whole situation was put into perspective. I was feeling courageous because I'd booked a flight and travelled to another part of the world without having met the person who was arranging my accommodation. Yet within 24 hours I'd met one group of people who took their lives into their own hands each day at work and another group of people who had gambled one month's salary and risked their lives in order to receive a charitable donation from me and the people I represented.

All of a sudden I realised who was heroic at that rehabilitation centre and it wasn't the guy who had brought a bag of free hands. Each and every one of the people who we were endeavouring to help had more courage in just going about their day-to-day lives than I did in my entire year. Not only are they forced to take more risks each day than I am. The nature of those risks is much more fundamental and often life-threatening.

At times we can seriously lose perspective in our privileged lives. We can somehow fool ourselves into thinking that changing the risk profile of our investment portfolio incorporates a degree of courage. We pump ourselves up to host friends and families for a barbeque and lay awake at night worrying about the best way to have a conversation with the people we love. Truly, the majority of things we worry about and are "forced" to overcome simply aren't material and wouldn't be considered even remotely challenging to some of the people I've met overseas.

As a business leader do you ever blow things out of proportion? Do you ever worry about matters that are ridiculously inconsequential in the scheme of things? Do you find yourself wasting time worrying about matters that are small and as a consequence running out of energy and courage to tackle some of those big issues?

When I was only 15, the notion of the "emotional bank account" was once explained to me in the context of building and maintaining healthy relationships with the people we love. To summarise the concept, all of us have an emotional bank account. When people do nice things for us, when they share positive experiences with us and when they make us feel loved they are effectively making a "deposit". When we fight with those people, experience emotional difficulties with them or feel betrayed then they are taking a "withdrawal". Research suggests that for a loving relationship to be maintained, the ratio of deposits to withdrawals needs to be at least five to one. Any less than that ratio we can still be friends but the genuine feeling of love tends to wane below that point.

Why am I talking about emotional bank accounts? I actually think that this metaphor is a useful concept when we're talking about courage within the workplace. If we all had "courage bank accounts" then the way to make deposits might be to invest in our sleep, health and well-being, develop strong empowering relationships, and seek out positive feedback. Each of those things is going to make us more resilient and less anxious about taking the odd risk. It's a deposit. Withdrawals would be every time that we take a risk, implement a courageous decision or worry about a decision that we've previously made. Withdrawals aren't bad things. You don't get a bank account to lock up your money forever and the same could be said of courage. I'd actually suggest that each time you make a courageous decision and experience success as a result you're making a deposit so you're capacity for courage increases over time.

What might we learn from the metaphor of the courage bank account? Although withdrawals aren't a bad thing in and of themselves, I think that too many of us spend all of our savings on the little things. We worry about day-to-day noise in our life and as a result we just don't have sufficient energy left for the BIG decisions that are waiting to be made in our lives. If you've been around work for long enough, someone has probably shared with you an incredibly useful and simple prioritisation model that divides things into those that are Important versus Unimportant and Urgent versus Not Urgent. The model is displayed below.

	Urgent	Not Urgent
Not Important	(3)	(4)
Important	(2)	(1)

The idea of this model is to literally list all of the "stuff" that takes up your time (or in this instance your courage). What do you worry most about? What decisions are most difficult for you? Each of those things is a withdrawal from your courage bank account and so should be listed in one of the four quadrants above. Of course if we were omnipotent and had unlimited emotional resources and time in our days then we would be able to invest in all of the things that you've included above. Sadly, we are not omnipotent (hate to break to it you) and we cannot, despite all of our best intentions, ever do everything so this model challenges us to prioritise Green, Blue and Yellow above Red. Although you will have to make choices from time to time to address unimportant yet urgent matters, many of those things do not warrant your emotional energy. That just leaves the Blue and Green quadrant and although they are separate they are obviously inextricably linked. Ultimately if you spend more time investing in Green then it stands to reason that the number of issues in the Blue box will reduce. As such, this model provides you with a natural way of prioritising the things that you want to invest your courage in.

If you want to be more courageous at work or in life in general you need to do three things:

(1) Make more deposits: Build resilience, invest in friendships, ensure that your prioritise your health and always get enough sleep.
(2) Limit withdrawals to only Green and Blue priorities
(3) Remember that you will grow your capacity for courage with increased success. It's a form of deposit... When you're starting out, choose Green and Blue priorities that are most likely to be successful.

When you pass away you WILL have some emails in your inbox that haven't been dealt with. The greatest leaders simply make a conscious decision about which things they prioritise and which they don't. They choose to ensure that there won't be any important emails left unattended. Let's learn a thing or two from the bravest people in the world - those that have courage simply because they don't have a choice. If you're lucky enough to have a choice about when and how you invest your courage then I'd encourage you to begin to take that opportunity without delay.

Chapter 15 – Key Insights

- Courage is a critical requirement for great leaders.
- We often waste our courage on stuff that doesn't matter.
- If we stop, pause and rethink we can all choose to invest our courage in ways that make the world a better place.

Chapter 16: Grace under pressure

I was raised being told every single day that I was special, loved and that there was nobody else like me in the entire world. It's one of the beliefs that I hold most dear and I think that many people reading this book also agree with that sentiment. That's why it can be so deeply confronting to us to know that many of the people around the world that are born with a disability or acquire one at some stage during their life believe that this disability is something to be ashamed of. I believe that each those people are also special, unique and capable of incredible things. However, unfortunately in some parts of the world people with a disability are told the exact opposite.

During my first trip to Cambodia I was working closely with one particular fellow who will remain nameless but I was working with him each and every day and he was helping with the fitting of hands. As is only natural, after a few days we were beginning to become very close friends and share stories about our family and loved ones. It was on the third day that we were working together that he revealed something that changed my whole perspective. He turned to me and lowered his voice and said, "You know some of these people probably deserve to be the way they are". I was shocked but asked another question before getting too upset with him. "Why is that?" I asked, the smile quickly disappearing from my face. He then went on to explain some religious beliefs that he held. Effectively he believed that some of the disabled folk who had lost hands might have stolen something in a past life and this was their punishment. I was upset with what he said but tried not to show this and simply said that I didn't agree with him. Each of us is of course free to believe what they want to believe and I didn't want to offend this man by challenging what might have been a deeply held religious conviction.

The people who receive a hand from us in South East Asia do not all grow up within communities that hold similar beliefs to my friend but sadly some of them do. I know that people who are missing a hand in the developing world are often ashamed of their disability. They will often go to great lengths to hide it. Maybe they'll where a long-sleeved shirt and tuck it into their trousers. Maybe they wear a long flowing sari. Either way, these people when in public are definitely trying to hide their disability. Often those people who are hiding their disability have learned to be invisible. Often they are personally in hiding and/or their families are hiding them away.

The idea of growing up in an environment where you are taught to be ashamed, taught that your disability is somehow your fault and taught that you should hide yourself away whenever possible is torturous to me. I cannot imagine growing up being taught all of those things without at some point having a deep level of resentment towards not only my family and friends but also myself. In short, I'm not sure how long I would last without self-harming. Yet that's not what I've experienced when I've had an opportunity to work with those very people. These people have learned to be invisible and taught to hide away their disability, yet here they are meeting a complete stranger and willing to be vulnerable enough to reveal their disability to me and ask for help. There is no resentment and afterwards the grateful thanks that are always genuinely heartfelt. These people are not aggressive or angry. I have no other way of describing it but they exhibit a level of graciousness that I could only dream of emulating myself.

One specific man comes to mind. He was the very first person to receive a hand as part of my first trip to Cambodia and was a double amputee. He had lost his hands digging irrigation canals for the Khmer Rouge decades ago and was unlucky enough to have an accident with the equipment at the time. Several years ago he had been lucky enough to be fitted with two hooks that enabled him to carry some objects more easily. When we fitted a hand to this man he hadn't held a pen for several decades. As soon as he put that pen in his new hand he began to write in the most perfect English. This was a very intelligent man who had been forced to live an invisible life. In that moment where we gave him a hand I like to think that we gave him much more than just a few additional physical abilities. I like to think that we gave him back a level of dignity that he previously didn't have. Once again though this is not a man that arrived at the rehabilitation centre grumbling and upset at his hooks. On the contrary he was deeply grateful for those devices. The humility with which this man obviously goes about his life and carries himself is something to truly be envied. He was one of the most dignified people I had ever met, despite being under circumstances that would have made him personally uncomfortable.

Another story that comes to mind was our trip to Bangalore in early 2014. Every year on January 2 a local rotary club in India holds what it calls the "Mega Limb Camp". It's critical that the camp is held in the same location and on the same date every year because so many of the people that come for assistance don't have fixed addresses or access to the internet. The camp relies heavily on word-of-mouth advertising to get the message out there and if those talking about the camp can confidently say that the camp is held at the same location every year at the same time it goes a long way towards helping ensure that the charity event is a big success each year.

The Mega Limb Camp is exactly what you might think it is. Effectively if you're missing a hand, foot or leg you can come and get a prosthesis for free. If you need crutches or callipers those are provided free of charge as well. During 2015 the group struggled to raise funds and didn't confirm that they would be able to proceed until the

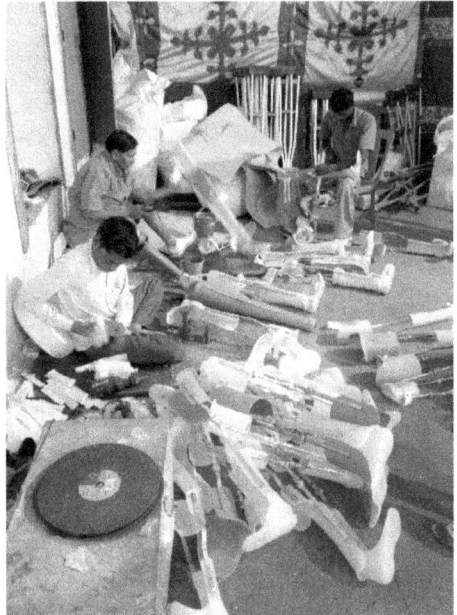

Callipers being assembled

last minute. Despite quite difficult circumstances, the 2015 Mega Limb Camp resulted in 517 people being provided with prosthetic legs, 933 people receiving callipers, 391 people receiving crutches and 59 people receiving new hands. This camp has now been run for 18 years in a row. It's truly inspiring what one small committed group can achieve when they put their mind to it. The event is held in the middle of Bangalore, India but people at times will travel several days to attend the event. Knowing this, the organisers don't just provide the immediate medical assistance that all attendees need, they go above and beyond by providing a place to sleep for the night and as many hot meals as they would like while they stay. This hospitality is not just extended to the people receiving a new leg or hand, it's also provided to their travelling companions and families.

When I attended the camp it was a truly amazing experience and when we didn't have any new recipients waiting for a hand I savoured the opportunity to check out everything else going on at the camp. The prosthetic legs given out at the camp are incredible. This part of the camp was run by the people from a charity called the "Jaipur Foot" (http://jaipurfoot.org/). Incredibly, this charity has provided 1.3million prosthetics to people in need since they were established in 1975.

The process to make a prosthetic leg is amazing. During the first step the recipient wraps their limb in Glad-wrap (shrink-wrap), a plaster cast is then produced which is an exact replica of the person's limb. This plaster cast obviously takes an hour or so to set and meanwhile some measurements are taken by the technician on duty. Once the cast is set, some plastic piping is then heated up within a standard pottery kiln before the technician then places the piping

Technicians hard at work

over the cast, then while wearing welding gloves they mould the plastic around the cast by hand. The final step is to round off the end of the pipe at the right length, insert a threaded nut, then screw on a pre-moulded foot (which comes in different sizes). End to end the process takes no more than 3 hours. In 3 hours, these prosthetics technicians make a completely tailored leg and then give it to their patient 100% for free then offer them a meal and accommodation – still for free.

Throughout the 3 hour process the recipients simply wait patiently (sometimes with shrink-wrap on their legs) while hundreds of people walk by. Perhaps their humility, and grace under difficult circumstances is

Moulded feet ready to be screwed onto a new leg

related to the fact that they are receiving such a valuable gift for free but I don't believe so. I believe that people in the developing world have no option but to depend on one another. They understand that they need their community and their community needs them. I'm certain that at least part of the reason they are able to receive our gifts so graciously is because of that more developed sense of community and knowledge of how important it is.

The first corporate job that I ever held was in Human Resources (HR). I was very good at my job and was quickly promoted. Unfortunately once that happened I was also quick to learn that terminating staff would be a big part of my role. It was also a very important part of my role. In the developed world it's rare that we are ever completely vulnerable while at work. Tragically, one of those times is often when we are being let go. The employee will arrive at a meeting with no pre-warning about what the meeting is about although the manager and HR Manager will have discussed and planned the details for days, sometimes weeks. A script is then often followed. The room will

179

have been chosen to hopefully minimise embarrassment for all concerned. The time of day and day of the week will have been investigated to ensure that birthdays and anniversaries are avoided and a taxi will be waiting nearby so as to ensure that the person gets home safely. It's a calculated affair because it needs to be. Although no termination is easy, the intent should always be to separate that employee with dignity and respect. In years to come although the person might not agree with the decision at least you want them to believe that you did everything you could to make the process as humane as it could be.

As an HR Manager you need to help your Manager adhere to good legal practices, you also need to be an advocate for a humane and dignified approach. It's a tricky situation to navigate and throughout the process a good HR Manager is able to remain in control of their emotions. They need to be the rational one whilst also being the moral compass for the business' decision maker. It's emotionally draining.

People who used to work with me would know that I coped by sometimes snapping at my co-workers and becoming a borderline workaholic. After a bit of self-reflection in about 2005 I took to taking 30 mins off after the process. Each time I let someone go I would visit a local tea shop and have a cup of tea. I would also buy a small packet of that tea and bring it back to my desk to try later. Since that role I have often half-joked that when I filled up my entire desk with boxes of tea I knew that it was time to leave that job. It didn't turn out to be a joke because sure enough, once that desk

180

was full 6 months later, I started looking at different options.

I often wonder what our recipients in the developing world would think about that most stressful period in my life. I was generously paid and I doubt that they would have had any sympathy for me. Perhaps they would have had sympathy for the people who I was separating until I explained what a typical severance package looked like. Research tells us that the most stressful experiences that we can experience are as follows:

- Death of a loved one
- Divorce
- Moving house
- Major illness
- Job Loss

Each of us will experience several of these stressors in our life-times, often at the most inconvenient of times. There is no shame in letting your guard down and feeling a bit more emotional during such a time. In fact, sometimes that is precisely what is required to help each of us recover and thrive after such an event.

I'm not about to suggest that we can all exhibit the kind of learned stoicism that defines many of poorest people in the world. The fact is that by merit of the very easy life that many of us has had we can't possibly hope to be as gracious under pressure as those people I've described and doing so might not be entirely healthy. Having said that, next time I experience one of these major stress events I'm going to do my very best to put that event in context. Chances are it won't be the end of the world and once the removalists have come and gone life just isn't going to be that bad.

If we each aspired to demonstrate the kind of graciousness under pressure that our friends overseas demonstrate I firmly believe that not only would we each be far better leaders in the workplace and community, but the world would also be a better place as a whole.

Chapter 16 – Key Insights

- Grace under pressure and humility are critical characteristics of inspired leaders.
- Good leaders practice putting things in perspective and don't waste energy on unimportant things.

Chapter 17: Forgiveness

It was about the third day of the Mega Limb Camp and Antonia and I had ducked off to share a quick meal with one of the main organisers of the Jaipur Foot project, Dr Ganesh. It was a quick meal as we were all keen to get back to the camp and continue our work. We returned to the camp and were greeted by two ladies. To be precise, one of the ladies seemed very keen to see us whereas the other lady was very quiet and rarely made eye contact. It was the quieter lady that was in need of a hand and throughout the registration process she was almost non-responsive. As a psychologist I would have described her has presenting with a "flat affect". She was not just unresponsive verbally but her non-verbal communication was also non-existent. At times it felt as though she was almost looking through us. By this stage in our trip we had fitted about 50 people with hands and most of those people didn't speak a word of English. Typically each recipient would speak via the translator that we had present and if they didn't speak to the translator they would at least look interested in the process. This lady was completely different.

The registration process for our hands is an important part of the process. Each person that receives a hand has their details recorded on a register and the process is primarily about good governance. When a group makes a hand in one of our workshops we promise that it will be given to someone in need and that person will not have to pay for it. Of course, we couldn't make such guarantees without recording some details about each person that receives a hand. One of the questions

183

that we always ask how they lost their hand. Sometimes the recipient will be too embarrassed to elaborate and will say something like "an accident". Whether this is a translation issue or genuine privacy we typically don't probe further. This lady was one of those people that fell into our "general accident" category of recipients.

After the registration process we then fit the hand to the recipient. During that process, we need to adjust the strapping that holds the hand to the residual limb. Everyone's arm is different but the strapping is incredibly versatile and can fit most limbs – it just takes some time to adjust everything. Of course the best way to help someone become comfortable with their new hand is to involve them in the process. Normally the recipient will become very interested during the process and we will ask them to help us by holding a strap here, pulling a strap there... anything that can help them understand how it all works. Throughout the process our friend was still relatively unresponsive. She was clearly watching our every move by this stage and did seem interested but was far from engaged in the process in the same way that everyone normally is.

Following the registration process practice is critical and ideally this is done in a group context. Each person will find different potential in the hand and will be instantly attracted to one or two functions over others. We typically find that in a group context each individual generates their own enthusiasm for different functions and ultimately everyone bounces off each other and becomes a lot more engaged in practicing as a result of doing it in a team environment. On this particular day our woman was the first to put on a hand after lunch and there was nobody else to practice with so we showed her a few basic functions. Typically we show each person at least four different ways to use their hand. The most common functions I like to explain include:

- Holding a pen
- Holding a toothbrush
- Using a shower sponge
- Holding a coffee mug
- Using cutlery

Our new recipient began to become engaged at this point and as soon as we showed her how to hold a mug she sat forward in her chair. It was the first sign of genuine enthusiasm that we'd seen so we went with it. We not only showed her how to hold the mug but we asked her to copy the process and try it on her own. She reached forward, grasped the handle lifted the mug to her lips, put the mug back on the table and released it then started crying. Of course nobody likes to see someone upset and we quickly asked her via the translator what was wrong. All of a sudden she was willing to communicate with us (instead of delegating that job to her friend). She explained that she did not want to come long to the Mega Limb Camp. She explained that she had lived her entire life without a hand and when she was a child she dreamt of receiving some assistance. However, following disappointment after disappointment she had taught herself to keep her expectations low. It was, as she said, her friend that made her come along as she didn't want to come along only to be disappointed again.

All of a sudden it all made sense: the unresponsiveness; the friend answering on her behalf; the solemn, almost vacant look in her eyes throughout the process. This woman had her walls up because she didn't want to be disappointed again. She was emotionally protecting herself in the same way that we all do when we've been hurt in the past.

At this point I ventured another question. "Would you mind if we asked you how old you were when you initially lost your hand?" I asked. "I was 3 years old" she replied with the help of a translator. "For 20 years I have been seeking this kind of assistance and taught myself that it was best to not have any hope". I ventured another question "How did you lose your hand?" but I was nowhere near prepared to hear her response. Our new hand recipient explained without hesitation that when she was three years old her father and uncle had become embroiled in a dispute. Her own uncle had actually cut off her hand on purpose as a way of seeking vengeance against her father. She was the most valuable property that the father owned and as such the uncle felt this was the best way of getting back at him.

Of course the notion of anyone being seen as someone else's property is nothing short of an affront on our basic humanity. It makes my skin crawl that women in many parts of the world are still seen as property by some men. It's even more troubling that slavery and human trafficking exists and by some measures is

186

actually quite prevalent to this day. However, putting these fundamental objections aside I'd like you to consider how this woman felt in that moment. For 20 years she has grown up believing that she is worth so little that her own family would mutilate her in that way. She's taught herself that this is how her life is going to be and that it is pointless of hoping for anything more. Then someone gave her a hand…

I like to think that in that moment we did much more than give that lady a hand. I think she experienced an emotional healing that was much more important than the physical hand we had given her. I think that in that moment, perhaps for the first time in her adult life she felt whole. In that moment you could also see her daring to perhaps hope again.

As we sat together we shared more and I learned that she was a seamstress by trade. Up until now her disability had not prevented her doing that job. She was able to handle the finer more dextrous functions required and with her residual limb she was able to help pull material through the machine. We found some material and showed her how the hand we gave her might be able to be useful and helped her grasp and pull the material with her new hand. She laughed and was not entirely convinced that her new hand would be any better than her residual limb for this purpose but that smile could have lit up the entire room.

I don't know how I would go on if one of my family members had violated my childhood in the way that this man had obviously done to this woman. I assume that at some stage during her life this lady not only needed to forgive her father but maybe also her uncle. It certainly sounded like she was still in contact with both men. I bet for much of her life she blamed herself for her injury and at some point needed to forgive herself.

We live in the most litigious age in history. If we suffer an injury or loss of any kind there are a range of advertisements encouraging us to take legal action to remedy the situation. Many legal firms will offer "no win no fee" remuneration structures so there are very few barriers to entry. While this whole approach does make it more likely that people are treated fairly I think it also prevents us from forgiving those that harm us.

Forgiveness is not just an act of grace towards another person, it's also a cleansing experience for both people concerned. Holding a grudge can not only eat up emotional energy it often holds us back from moving on. Can you think of a person who you have never forgiven for a past indiscretion or wrong that committed against you? Can you think of anything you're personally ashamed of in your past? Now, think of how many times you reflect on either of those things. Ask yourself not only the amount emotional energy that you've burned on this issue in the past, but also whether you've chosen against taking up a new opportunity as a result? We've all done it. Maybe it was a foregone coffee with a friend just in case someone else happened to be there. Maybe we didn't trust ourselves in a particular environment so said no to a promotion or new opportunity. Please trust me when I say that there is no grudge, even a self-inflicted one, that has ever helped someone move forward in their life and if our hand recipient can forgive her father and herself for chopping off her hand then I'm pretty sure that you CAN let go of whatever you're holding onto right now.

Forgiveness is the kind of concept that we expect to be discussed during a sermon or maybe during an Oprah interview. However, it's equally important in the workplace. I still remember one really disappointing period during my career where I had been turned back for a role that I felt I deserved. I'd actually been acting in the role for 9 months and been doing all but killing myself to do the job. I remember frequently still being in the office at midnight and by the time Friday came around I was so exhausted that I would normally go home and watch TV. I resented this quite a bit because at the time I was only in my mid 20s and was a single man. I would have loved to be in a relationship but frankly never put myself in a situation where I might meet someone. Despite this I felt it would all be worth it if I got that promotion.

When I was called into a meeting with my manager to learn that I hadn't received the job it was upsetting enough but when I found out who had been successful it was like I had been stabbed in the heart. Throughout the job application process I had been quite close to my previous manager and had confided a lot in her. I'd also asked for her advice throughout the preparation of my application and she'd encouraged me. At no point did she disclose that she had applied for that role so when I didn't secure that promotion I also felt like I had lost a friend. I felt deeply betrayed.

I look back at that whole situation now and am pleased that I was unsuccessful. I know that my life would have stayed on a particular path if I'd received that promotion. Sure I might be earning a lot of money right now but I think that I would be unhappy by almost every other measure. I also wouldn't have achieved any of the things that I hold most dear right now. Perhaps I wouldn't even have met my now wife! By every measure it was the best thing that could have happened to me however I recently bumped into the person that received that promotion up at my local supermarket. She apparently lives within a block or two of me and we had a very brief chat. On the way home, I found myself explaining to my wife the whole situation. I even found myself explaining how within 6 months of taking the role my ex-friend hadn't been able to cope and hired 3 additional staff to help perform the job. Effectively they had replaced me with 4 different people and then lost the best asset in their team. My rant took a solid ten to fifteen minutes and I remember feeling genuinely distressed as I sat back down at the television focussed on nothing but a mental score-board about who had ended up better in the long-run.

In that moment, my heart was filled with nothing but hate. I wasn't able to help prepare dinner in a meaningful way and I doubt that my wife would have wanted me to help as I was super grumpy. Ten years later and although I've moved on from the situation I still hadn't forgiven my friend. To be honest I also hadn't forgiven myself for working so hard during that period in my life and effectively losing a couple of years of my youth. It can be so difficult to forgive. I should know. However, it's the only way to truly move on. In ten years, I can't think of a single positive thing that has happened to me as a result of keeping a scar on my heart from a relatively trivial workplace situation. It's just not worth it. Forgiving others is truly the only way to move on and reach your full potential as a leader.

Chapter 17 – Key Insights

- Holding a grudge in life rarely creates value for anyone.
- The workplace is no different and often long-term grudges hold us back emotionally.
- Forgiveness is a critical practice for every leader.
- It is possible to hold a grudge against yourself. Often the most important first person to forgive is yourself.

Chapter 18: Generosity and Divestism

One of the most touching stories I've received from the field is the story of the first man to receive a hand in Hyderabad, India. I have not personally gone to Hyderabad but this story was relayed to me by a group of Rotarians who have been very successful in fitting our hands onto people all over that city. As the story goes, this gentleman was the first of many waiting in line to receive a hand at the very first fitting camp. He was friendly and courteous (as I've found most people in India to be) but there was nothing outstanding or striking about him except the fact that he was an amputee and his residual limb was perfectly suited to our hand.

As per our normal process, the recipient was registered, had his hand fitted, then provided with some instructions and given a chance to practice. He then left the camp wearing his new hand and a big smile. There was nothing striking about this particular man and the fitting team eagerly moved onto the next recipient.

Several months passed and our Rotarian friends held another event to provide hands to people in need. Once again this same man was at the front of the line and he was no longer wearing his hand. Our teams need to investigate these kinds of situations carefully. When our clients build and pay for each hand to be distributed we undertake to ensure that each hand finds its way to someone in need and that person will never have to pay a cent for their gift. We believe that this is a solemn pledge that we're making to each and every client and we take that pledge seriously. If this man had earned some extra money by selling his hand and was attempting to pull the wool over our eyes then we need to know about it. So our people gently interrogated him but when they heard his story they were flabbergasted.

You see this man had only owned his hand for about 2 hours. As he was travelling home from the fitting camp, he was walking along the street and came across a young mum with no arms and two kids. He was overwhelmed by the generosity he had experienced from our team earlier in the day and wanted to "pay it forward." The best way he knew how was to give his hand to this woman because in his mind she clearly needed it more than he did. That is why he was back seeking another hand.

Often it is the poorest in our community, those of us that have the least, that are the most generous with what they have. This man probably only had 2 or 3 sets of clothes. He had travelled several hours to receive a hand that was going to potentially help him secure a job, feed and clean himself more easily and provide him some additional dignity. By any stretch of the imagination that hand was his most prized possession at that specific time. Yet he gave it away without hesitation.

Religious scholars have long posited the perils of wealth. Typically, they have cautioned that materiality effectively holds people back. When you purchase a new set of clothes or a sports car it makes you feel great in the short term but it's like a sugar hit. As soon as the

193

sugar wears off, you're checking out the next winter collection or latest model car. Happiness via material possessions is simply not a sustainable way to find lasting satisfaction and inner-peace. I wonder, there isn't something we can all learn for those people who have nothing in the world, yet are the most generous with what they have.

I believe that our society is at the start of a fundamental shift in the way that we see ownership and the world in general. It is a shift that has already begun to influence people at work and will likely do so for many years to come. However, it's not just a shift in the way that we see our workplaces, but also our physical possessions, our environment and our relationships. I call it *"Divestism"* and it goes to the heart of how our world is beginning to change its views on ownership.

Nineteen years ago I bought a Lenny Kravitz album. It was only about the tenth CD that I had ever owned and I LOVED it. So did a couple of my friends and one day one of them borrowed the album, left it on his dashboard in the sun and overnight the CD was ruined. Although I loved the album, I had also listened to it hundreds of times and I simply could not afford to replace it (CD's were more expensive back then) and to this day I have never bought a replacement copy of that specific album. Sometimes owning stuff isn't all that it cracked up to be.

I have just purchased an Apple TV. It's an amazing device. For those who have not seen one, it's a very small box that you plug into your television. It also connects to your wireless internet and basically enables you to download and watch any movie, TV show or music that's ever been made and stream it to your television. You have to pay for the privilege of course but this little box effectively makes your local video shop redundant. Perhaps the thing that makes me most excited about my new toy is the fact that if I buy something on my Apple TV it is immediately available on my iPhone, iPad and computer via iTunes. I still own all the videos and music that I've bought but I don't own anything that I can physically hold in my hands. In the past, this might have been seen as a limitation, but as I look at the big pile of DVDs under my TV taking up space I can't help but challenge that assumption.

The fact is that the vast majority of kids these days will never experience the sadness of losing a CD like the one I did (and not just because they don't listen to Lenny Kravitz anymore). Every CD they buy will be stored in the "cloud" and be instantly accessible for the rest of their lives. They'll be immune from the impact of changes in technology, scratched records and even hot car dashboards. Although they won't own a physical asset like we did, they will also be free from the burden of those assets. CDs and DVDs are just the beginning of this trend. People are doing way more than just storing their movies in the "cloud". As the internet gets faster, it is becoming possible to access software and do some seriously powerful computing remotely. There will come a time (in the not so distant future) where we will no longer need to configure all our software on our local computers or even download those pesky updates. In fact some futurists suggest that the concept of a Personal Computer will become

195

redundant relatively soon due to this technology. You remember… that thing that transformed the last couple of decades… it'll become ancient history soon!

Now before you think that this trend is confined to the technology and entertainment sector, lets consider two of the holy grails of ownership… the family home and car. If you're like me, you owe a small fortune on your home. Most of us were raised to aspire to home ownership and worked hard to achieve that goal. However, we were also raised to assume perpetual double-digit growth in the value of that home and our expectations just haven't been realised. Yet the mortgage still has to be paid. I still love owning my own home and have no regrets about buying it. However, the fact is, more people nowadays are starting to take a different perspective. A recent survey in Mortgage Magazine recently published a survey that showed 52% of first home buyers saying that they would consider being a life-long renter. Similarly, although owning a car was never seen as an investment, it was seen as core to a western way of life. It enabled our independence, it meant we could go anywhere at any time. For most of us it still does. However, have you noticed recently the number of share car spaces located throughout our cities and most populated suburbs. People are even beginning to change their attitudes towards owning a car. Most people aren't abandoning their cars altogether but there are certainly a number of people that are choosing a share car scheme for their second car and when husband and wife are needing to travel in different directions, they just borrow a share car for a few hours.

The trend towards "Divestism" isn't just confined to the physical world. Let's get a bit more personal and talk about relationships. Not only will kids nowadays NEVER lose touch with their schoolmates thanks to Facebook and similar websites, but they can keep in touch without physically going to a school reunion or coffee with a friend. The basis of many of their relationships will be fundamentally intangible. Yet in many ways their relationships will be more productive and connected than the generations that have gone before them. The way relationships are changing is at the essence of *"Divestism"*. Not convinced that relationships have changed in the last decade? Let's consider for a second that the whole meaning of the term "friend" has evolved from being a noun to both a verb and a noun. To "friend" someone on Facebook has a very real meaning to anyone who is active on social networking and not only can you friend someone easily nowadays but you can also defriend them with the click of your mouse. This might seem fickle to some but social networking has fundamentally changed the way people see relationships. This is best illustrated by the social trend that to "make a relationship official" almost universally refers to updating your relationship status on Faccbook nowadays. The immaterial or insubstantial is becoming increasingly important to people as the trend continues.

So how could *"Divestism"* have permeated so many parts of our lives without impacting on our workplaces? The fact is it has already had a major impact on the way people see employment, their workplace and their manager. Nowadays employees

197

are looking for more than money and job security. They are looking for challenge, for a sense of purpose and for autonomy. If employees don't find what they are looking for from their employer they are more confident to leave their workplaces and find another job. Better still, they are willing to work casually, to work for themselves, to have multiple jobs or even invent their own jobs via the internet (or something else that hasn't been invented yet).

None of these workplace changes are new. The vast majority of business leaders have acknowledged all of the trends that I've referenced above. However, I would argue that most have fundamentally misdiagnosed the problem. *"Divestism"* is a game-changer. It's a trend that cannot be stopped and businesses that do not fundamentally change the way they do business as a result will be putting themselves in a precarious position. To assume that skills shortages will lessen with the ebbs and flows of the economic cycle, that you can retain employees by ensuring that you give out salary increases greater than inflation, or that you can negotiate outcomes with unions that will universally be accepted might all be good precautions to take. However, these measures are necessary without being sufficient. In order to retain employees, workplaces need to engage with their people on a deeper level. They need to get beyond the material and understand what truly drives their people. They also need to listen to what they learn.

When you think about it, the very terms "Human Resources" or "Human Capital" imply a sense of false ownership. They imply that people are assets that are owned just like the rest of the company's physical assets. I understand that this has been an incredibly useful metaphor over the past 40 years. It's helped HR folk justify investment in valuable programs or initiatives. However, although these are both relatively modern terms, they still hark back to the days when people would follow instructions unquestioningly, when lifelong employment was a goal for most people and when people would cope with significant hardships in order to achieve that goal.

If the trend towards *"Divestism"* continues at current rates, then companies that cling to the notion of people as assets or resources will be left behind. In the future, companies must accept that people will weave in and out of employment; that they never truly own their employees and realign their people-related investments accordingly. The companies that truly realign their people systems with the concept of *"Divestism"* will not necessarily adopt a "retain at all costs" mentality to their people. When their employees part ways with their employer, progressive companies will see this as the first step in attracting them back. They might even support past employees in pursuing their goals outside of employment under some circumstances. The lines between employee, customer, spokesperson, advocate, sponsor and supplier are also likely to blur further with people-related investments justified beyond traditional departmental boundaries. Future editions of our newsletter will explore the specific implications of *"Divestism"* for business. However, needless to say its implications are broad.

The core of *"Divestism"*, as I define it, is that at this time in the world's history, the less obvious, the subjective and intangible aspects of the world, are becoming more highly valued than they ever have been before. Ownership is clearly less valued and perceived as a burden to some. It's an exciting time to be alive, but it's also a risky time to hold onto old paradigms whilst running a business.

Chapter 18 – Key Insights

- The value of material wealth is often over-rated.
- True selfless generosity will always inspire others.
- Inspired leaders enable their people to run their own race and do not pretend that they own their people.
- Inspired cultures are places where employees weave in and out of their employment. They are never owned and work there because they want to.

Chapter 19: Humanising our goals and achievements.

Both of our charity projects incorporate an artwork and photography activity. Within Helping Hands, participants build their prosthetic before then decorating the carry case it comes in. Participants are challenged to think about what they want to communicate with their end recipient and capture that in a graphical format. Of course the end recipient of each hand rarely speaks English so the artwork truly is each team's most valuable opportunity to look into their hearts and communicate something with the person they are helping. Once each group finishes their artwork project they are then asked to take a photo of their group proudly displaying their artwork and then email that photo through to us. When we receive the photo in our email we print it out and place it with that group's artwork. Our Water Works activity is similar but effectively groups decorate an artwork slate that they get to keep. We take a copy of that artwork, convert it into a sticker and decorate the water filtration system that is donated on their behalf with the unique artwork that each group produced. The process is facilitated by a website called www.3billionstories.com which effectively tracks the progress of each gift and ensures that the sponsors are provided with a photo of the family, school or medical centre that received their gift. Of course with Helping Hands, the decoration is only used on the protective case that the hand comes in so might not be looked at on a daily basis whereas the water filtration system that is donated is utilised every day and normally takes pride of place within the family's home or yard.

From time to time, I have workshop participants ask me if they really have to do the artwork activity. This request is never motivated by malice. Normally such people are just afraid of being let loose with permanent markers for the first time since they were a kid. Typically they are so motivated by a desire to do a good job for their end recipient that they are scared of drawing something that might not be perfect. I always encourage those people who ask this question to definitely get involved for two very good reasons:

(1) The first reason is not the most important one but is still critical. Many of us non-artists in the world turn our back on that part of us at a relatively young age. Maybe we didn't enjoy drawing. Maybe we were embarrassed that we weren't naturally as gifted as the person next to us and gave up trying. Perhaps we didn't think it was "cool" or we were told it was "silly" to indulge such a pastime when we should be out there forging a career.

The fact is that we are genetically all very similar. We each have a part of the brain that is not just partial to artistic pursuits, it's the sole reason it's there. I remember really clearly a situation about 10 years ago now. I was in the middle of studying for my Masters in Organisational Psychology at the time so was studying hard every night with very little time for relaxation. I also had been working in the same career for quite a while and it was a very analytical job. I rarely had an opportunity to indulge my creative side and to be frank had forgotten that I even had one. The one day someone made me go along to an art class at a local pub. I laugh now when I think about it because doing an art class at the local pub was probably the only way that someone could have convinced me to try out such a thing. Having said that the results were almost instant. As soon as I picked up that piece of charcoal and started sketching I was in a different world. After 60 minutes I felt this intense sense of relaxation even though I'd been concentrating for a solid hour. At the time without having to think about it I just knew that I was engaging a part of my brain that had not had a chance to be used for years. In that moment I reconnected with my creative side and realised how limited my own view of myself was. It didn't matter whether or not my charcoal drawings were any good. That was entirely beside the point.

Of course decorating a hand carrying case with coloured markers is not exactly the same situation as what I've described above but I do know that there are people who have gotten a lot out this component of the activity. Both Helping Hands and Water Works are about helping to wake people up and see the world from a different perspective. The artwork component of both activities just helps incorporate an additional perspective that most participants don't expect.

(2) The second, and most important reason is to humanise the gift that we're giving. We want to ensure that each person that gets to be a part of the activity feels closer to their end recipients even though they are on the other side of the world. In addition, we want to communicate in the simplest way possible to the end recipient that this is the group that made the hand and what better way than to send a photo with a group clearly holding exactly the same carry case as the one you've just been given. Even without speaking the same language or having a competent translator, the artwork component of this activity ensures that each and every recipient is crystal clear about why they are receiving this donation, who made the hand for them and also that those people wish them nothing but the best.

Humanising the gifts that we give as part of the program is potentially the most critical aspect of our workshop design. We don't want people to just feel emotional and good about themselves when they participate (although that's one of our clear goals), we also want to make sure that the person at the other end of genuinely appreciates the gift and understands where it came from. I always think it's a bit funny when people are shocked by this. It's rare that they would say it out-loud but I know that many people secretly believe people in poverty should be unquestionably grateful for anything they are given. It's the typical perspective of someone who doesn't understand that poor people are no different to rich ones. We are all just a cacophony of emotions, thoughts, interests, beliefs and values. We are all the same. If you're like me, you're probably far less likely to utilise a free sample that someone gives me as you're getting off the train in the morning than you are to use something you've spent my hard-earned money on. There's just something about free stuff. Sometimes we don't trust it. Sometimes we accepted it even though we knew we didn't need it. Almost always, we value it less than something we have paid for.

When we send a photograph of three people holding a hand with a decoration that they have clearly done themselves and you can see in the eyes of those people how excited and proud they are of what they are doing. That's when we make that hand so much more than just a free product sample we picked up while getting on the train in the morning. All of a sudden that free stuff becomes a gift from the heart. All of a sudden our recipients see the hand for what it is and are motivated to learn how to use it and get maximum value out of it.

I've spoken previously about the dignity of those folk waiting calmly in Bangalore for their new prosthetic legs. These people were typically sitting in a row with one or two other people with their legs still wrapped in plastic. During this time, they are not in a formal, private waiting room. That just wouldn't have been possible as there were no rooms whatsoever at our camp, just many tents all arranged in an orderly fashion. The only tent that had a degree of privacy as you would expect was the one that was set-up as the overnight accommodation for anyone that chooses to sleep there before returning home. Those leg recipients would wait patiently seated on several pre-arranged chairs. The chairs were laid out near the prosthetics station so that they could observe their prosthetic being manufactured however it was also positioned in a pinch-point geographically where literally hundreds of people would pass each hour going from one part of the camp to another. Talk about grace under pressure.

Of course these dignified individuals were not just a product of their upbringing but they were also working with a team of prosthetics technicians that clearly had their heart in the right place. Those technicians were working furiously and there wasn't a time that I didn't see one of those individuals with sweat on their brow. They were reaching into a red-hot kiln wearing nothing but welding gloves on their hands. They were personally pushing themselves to cope with the extreme discomfort of such hot work within an environment where it was above 30 degrees Celsius (about 92 degrees Fahrenheit). Their customers were people with no financial means to pay for their services. They were going to receive their legs for free but still those prosthetics technicians worked furiously to do a good job. You could tell in just a glance that each and every prosthetic technician took their job very personally and that each leg had to be perfect before it was completed. There's no doubt in my mind that the

206

way these technicians carried themselves helped create an environment where their recipients felt that they were in good hands.

All of those facts, striking as they might be, are trumped by one final observation. Every single one of those prosthetics technicians was walking around on a leg that they had received from the Jaipur Foot project. They weren't just employed to help change the lives of others. They were once customers who now had jobs as a result of the gift they had been given. They were living, breathing examples of what could be achieved as a result of one of these prosthetics. They were also able to deeply empathise and connect which each one of their customers in a way that I simple could not have done.

Recipient of a new leg

Meaningful work is so central to each and every person's psychological well-being. As much as we remember how blissful it might have been as teenagers to sleep in until 1pm, we're actually all born wanting to have something that gets us out of the bed in the morning. Work gives us a sense of order and structure for our day. Most of us spend the majority of our waking hours at work and as a result our social network is inextricably linked to the workplace. The people we depend on for support are often our colleagues, just as much as they are our family members. Many people would not even distinguish between family and their friends at work; the two are one and the same.

My very first full-time job in the city was a really exciting time for me. I would travel into town each day with all of the other commuters via the train. I wasn't dreaming big at that stage. There was no pressure to progress. I just wanted to be accepted. I wanted to look like I deserved the job and was smart enough to be there. I also have to admit that I just really enjoyed the novelty of going into the city each day. One of my habits was to go and have lunch in a local food-court that was nearby and each day I went there I would see an older gentlemen dressed in a suit with his briefcase on the chair next to him. He was always there before I arrived and after I left. After a week or so I had cause to visit that food-court for morning tea. I was having coffee with a colleague and we also had to purchase a birthday card for a colleague at a nearby newsagent. Once again that older gentleman was sitting in the same place, in the same suit with that same briefcase. I could well be completely wrong but I'm pretty certain that this man had lost his job but hadn't yet built up the courage to tell his family. Maybe he had shared the news with his family but still valued the routine of going to the same place every day. Either way, it deeply saddened me however it also emphasised the importance all of us place on work.

I think that we all yearn to have the kind of passion for our work that each of those prosthetics technicians do. Even if the work that we do isn't so obviously humanistic, I think that we all long for a similar sense of purpose and social connection at work. Human beings are inherently social creatures. Even those of us that pride ourselves on being very data-driven, by the book people yearn to feel accepted and to make a difference for others.

When you compress a strong spring it might not give much resistance at first. It will initially allow you to do what you want with it. However as you exert more and more pressure it becomes increasingly inevitable that eventually it will expand back to its original form. Of course you could take to the spring with a set of bolt-cutters or destroy it in any number of ways however then it ceases to ceases to still be a spring. Human beings are inherently good creatures. We are social beings. We want to help others and to make a difference and if a workplace makes us behave contrary to that for a short period of time we can cope with it in the short-term. However, you can't take the humanity out of a person without destroying what made them human in the first place. Why would you want to do that?

In the workplace we have a funny way of pretending that we're not dealing with human beings. When we're putting together our budget or commencing our business planning cycle too often the people aspects of that process are seen as just one workstream or worse-still, ignored altogether. The reality is that every aspect of your business plan and strategy is underpinned by people. It's not one of the pillars holding up your roof. It's the foundation of your building. It underpins the stability of every other aspect of your plan.

During the industrial revolution, amidst the emergence of the production line, people were often seen in a similar way to machines. We conducted time and motion studies to determine the most effective ways to divide up tasks and then tried to define jobs in such a detailed fashion as to eliminate all discretion from the job. Although production lines and time and motion studies still have their place in some contexts, such notions are patently ridiculous in the majority of modern workplaces. I would challenge you to find many people that disagree with such a statement. Yet I believe we continue to try and construct our workplaces as if eliminating the humanity, creativity and emotion from our workplaces is a worthwhile pursuit. It simply is not.

Prior to reading this book, how long would you have thought it might take to build a functional prosthetic leg that not only was high quality but also tailored to the specific shape of each individual's residual limb and was made of rigid plastic? Would you have guessed that the process might take Months? Weeks? Days? The process takes three hours. If I had not seen it with my own eyes I wouldn't even think such a thing was imaginable yet it is and there are over 1 million people who can attest to the quality of the product.

Humanising the workplace is not just a nice thing to do. It's critical. Thinking about and investing in initiatives that help our employees connect on an emotional level with their customers and other co-workers is critical if you are to observe your team reaching its full potential. We are all deeply emotional and social creatures and the second your leadership style begins to indulge the idea that we are not should be the second that you start to plan for underwhelming results in your workplace.

Chapter 19 – Key Insights

- People care about "People" far more than they care about "Stuff"
- Engagement is an emotional construct and if you want people to truly care about the work that they do then workplace goals should be related back to the difference that you're making to people wherever possible.

IV.　　WHERE TO FROM HERE?

When I first started writing this book I set-out to answer the question "As leaders what are some of the most important things we can learn from people living in the developing world?" This book was not meant to be an exhaustive dissertation on global poverty, cultural change or leadership it was just a sample of stories that I hoped would help each reader see the world from a different perspective. The limitations of my analysis are many and varied but if I have given you just one or two major insights that might prompt you thinking about the world in a slightly different way, my work here is done.

I am sure that each reader will take something slightly different from this book, however my hope is that after reading we can all agree on several key principles:

1. Everyone on the planet was born for a reason. We all have both the potential and responsibility to create positive waves in the world. To leave this place better than what we found it. We are all potential leaders waiting for an excuse to step-up into our destiny.

2. There is lot that we can learn from people living in the developing. If we are willing to humbly reflect on and learn from the stories that I've shared together we could transform modern workplaces.

3. Too often we let the inconsequential rule our life. There are things in this world that are worth

worrying about however too often we lose perspective and let day-to-day irritants determine the course of our lives.

4. We should all do our very best to help those less fortunate in the world. Although we each have different ways of going about this we all have a responsibility to chip in and help make our global community a better place for all of its inhabitants.

This book would not be possible without the countless people I've encountered overseas whose stories I've shared with you. Those stories are in some instances deeply personal and often confronting. I hope that we can do service to those stories by continuing to fund the work we do via the Helping Hands and Water Works projects. By purchasing this book you have played a big part in enabling us to do just that.

Now that you've read this book, my hope is that you will continue to honour the stories I've shared by *being the change that you want to see in the world.*

www.ingramcontent.com/pod-product-compliance
Lightning Source LLC
Chambersburg PA
CBHW030416100426
42812CB00028B/2978/J